Stressed Out

Strategies for Living and Working in Corrections

2nd Edition

Gary F. Cornelius

American Correctional Association
Lanham, Maryland

Mission of the American Correctional Association

The American Correctional Association provides a professional organization for all individuals and groups, both public and private, that share a common goal of improving the justice system.

Printed in the United States of America by United Graphics Inc., Mattoon, Il.

ISBN: 1-56991-223-8

This publication may be ordered from:
American Correctional Association
4380 Forbes Boulevard
Lanham, Maryland 20706-4322
1-800-222-5646

For information on publications and videos available from ACA, contact our worldwide web home page at: http://www.aca.org

Library of Congress Cataloging in Publication Data

Cornelius, Gary F.

  Stressed out! : Strategies for living and working with stress in corrections/Gary F. Cornelius.—2nd ed.
    p. cm.
  Includes bibliographical references.
  ISBN 1-56991-223-8 (pbk.)

Correctional Personnel—Job stress—United States. 2. Stress (Psychology)—United States. I. American Correctional Association. II. Title

HV9470.C67 2005

365'.01'9—dc22   2004062659

Table of Contents

Appendices

Dedication

This book is dedicated to my late wife Nancy, who always believed in me. She is gone from us now, but her love and guidance remains. She was a guiding influence in my life.

I also dedicate it to our children, Gary Jr., and Amber Beth. They also believed in my mission to share my knowledge and experiences with the present and future generations of corrections workers.

Thank you all.

Gary F. Cornelius

Acknowledgments

The author wishes to thank the following institutions, staff, and individuals who were very helpful in the production of this work:

Arlington County, Viriginia, Detention Center: Major Mike Pinson, Captain Dave Kidwell, and Lieutenant Vicki Bandalo

Fairfax County, Virginia, District 29 Probation and Parole: Leslie Bubenhofer, Chief Probation Officer, and staff.

Clarke-Frederick-Winchester Regional Adult Detention Center, Fred Hildebrand, Superintendent, and Lieutenant Patty Barr

John Carr, Executive Director, Family Service Society

Mecheal Dedeian: Senior Probation and Parole Officer, Norfolk, Virginia, Probation and Parole

Peggy Thompson, Probation and Parole Officer, District 29, Fairfax, Virginia.

Bill Hauser, U.S. Probation Officer, Clearwater, Florida.

Dorothy Wine, Rehabilitation Counselor

William Hepner, New Jersey Department of Corrections

Marlene Koopman, Iowa Department of Corrections

Special thanks go to the George Mason University Human Emotions Research Lab for their assistance in the stress questionnaire and statistics:

Dr. June Tangney, Director

Jeff Pattison, Assistant

GFC

Preface

Stress is a widely used buzzword that we in corrections have heard many times throughout our careers. Our colleagues and families have said: "he is under a lot of stress," or "that last incident up on the tier—that really stressed her out." Or—"Dan quit because he couldn't take the stress and got 'burned out.'" Corrections is one the most stressful occupations. Stress is an inherent part of this occupation. In the past decade and a half, more information has been published about stress in corrections. Stress training and programs have come a long way.

Bookstores and grocery-store checkout aisles are full of books and magazines that describe all types of stress-management techniques. We are in an information age. We have videotapes, the Internet, and cable television with hundreds of channels conveying the message that people can live healthy lifestyles and reduce stress.

However, this is not just another book on stress management. This is a book originally published in 1994, which has been extensively updated from its original edition, for one group of people—the men and women who are the correctional professionals of this nation. This group includes, but is not limited to the correctional officer, the probation officer, the parole officer, the counselor, correctional health care staff, the juvenile care worker, and so on. These workers strive under limited resources and staffing to keep our society safe by providing correctional services.

This book is designed to help the many people who work in corrections enjoy longer, healthier lives and careers by learning how to manage stress in their everyday life. It is written by a corrections worker with more than twenty-five years of experience, a worker who has seen colleagues under stress, has experienced stress, and has learned to manage it. Hopefully, this book will help you do the same.

Gary F. Cornelius
January 2005

Foreword

We are very pleased to be publishing this second edition of Gary Cornelius' thoughtful work on stress management. It provides some time-tested and some novel methods for reducing the stress of those working in corrections. As a lieutenant at the Fairfax County (Va.) Jail, he has seen his share of stressed-out officers and personnel and the potential problems that can arise when stress is left unchecked. While undertaking the revision of this text, he contacted people across the nation in all branches of correction—prisons, jails, probation and parole, and juvenile facilities and asked them about their stressors. This cross-comparison of stressors in corrections provides a unique perspective on the problem.

Stress and its management is not only a concern to the corrections professional but to the management of the correctional agency. Stress can lead to increased health problems, which, in turn, result in extra time off or staff being unfit for their duties. Cornelius documents how stress leading to burnout can cause conditions to be unsafe for the rest of the staff who must work around the stressed-out person who is not performing his or her duties in an optimal manner. Then, he goes further and shows what correctional supervisors can do to help lower the stress level of those they supervise. He also offers some practical help for those with post traumatic stress syndrome.

Of course, he provides some practical and immediate ways for individual staff members to cope and lower their stress. After all, he's been there and knows what types of stresses correctional officers and staff face both on and off the job. And, don't skip the appendices in this work—they are full of positive suggestions that are easy to implement.

We wish you well in your corrections career. Because it cannot be stress-free, we offer this book to help you navigate the path to less stress and a happier life.

James A. Gondles, Jr., CAE
Executive Director
American Correctional Association

Introduction

There are demands on us in everyday life—the bills come due, the car needs service, the kids are sick, or you just don't feel like going to work today. Coupled with these demands are the careers that we have chosen: working with probationers, parolees, working a floor in a jail, or in a tower in a maximum-security prison. Maybe you are a juvenile counselor or a prison medical officer. It seems at times that correctional work makes our lives more difficult. We feel the stress.

Many citizens think that all jail officers do is to count inmates or turn keys in a lock. The public thinks that all probation officers do is to call offenders into their office. Common wisdom is that juvenile counselors reign in incorrigible youths. Not true—we in corrections know that our jobs are composed of much more than that. Dealing with the demands of corrections: the inmates; the clients; security problems; shift work; short staffing; risk of death; injury or disease; to name a few, seem to take a lot out of us.

Corrections is a dynamic, unpredictable, and ever-changing field. It is a tough job, sometimes made tougher as we try to live a positive life while we work in a negative field. This book hopefully will give correctional workers new ways to deal with stress, and the results will be happier lives, better health, and longer careers. It is plainly written, blunt in some places, but its central theme is to get you to think and make changes. A career in corrections should not make you feel sick, rob you of the wonderful things that life has to offer, or make you die before your time.

The goals of this updated work are as follows. The reader will:

- Become aware of recent information concerning stress and health
- Learn what stress is, how it affects us, both physically and mentally
- Learn how recent developments in corrections are correlated to workers' stress levels
- Learn proven, effective stress-coping techniques both on and off the job
- Learn better ways to manage time
- Obtain information on how other corrections workers and agencies are dealing with stress, including information on peer counseling and agency programs
- Learn how to develop a personalized stress-management plan

This work gives the corrections professional a proactive approach to stress—it teaches us how to stay healthy physically and mentally in an occupation that seems to drain us at times. Also, it will explore what to do in a crisis when the stress and strain become overwhelming. Both approaches are important. They prepare the worker to deal with stress—both the day-to-day type and the serious-incident type. As reported by the late Frances Cheek, a pioneer researcher in corrections stress, studies show that the average lifespan of a correctional officer was only fifty-nine years—too short and too tragic. Cheek also reported research indicating the effects of stress in correctional officers: alcohol abuse, divorce, physical problems, and emotional problems (Cheek, 1984).

In developing this book, the author contacted several corrections agencies for information and took pictures at several others. Also, the author sent a "grassroots" questionnaire to corrections workers to find out both what are some stressors and what workers are doing to cope. Much of the information throughout this book has been updated based on this questionnaire and the latest scientific research.

The road to stress management, like other hurdles in life, starts with a single step. It is time to change. This book can help you be prepared both physically and mentally to deal with a stressful occupation and lessen the toll it takes on your life. Let this book give you a gentle "nudge" to get ready.

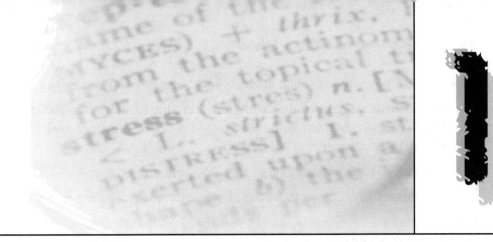

Stress: What Is it?

After reading this chapter, you should understand the following:

- What stress is
- How stress and the stress cycle affects us
- The differences between negative and positive stressors
- How we mentally and physically react to stress

Stress is and has been for the past several decades a concern for any of us who want to live a physically and mentally healthy lifestyle. In the 1980s, stress-related mental disorders were contributing to what was called the fastest growing occupational disease (Poe, 1987).

Even though we now know more about stress, and programs and techniques that are available to help us deal with it, things could be better. To understand the cost of stress, physically, mentally, and financially, read the following composite of recent studies including those from the Gallup Organization, Intregra, the National Institute of Occupational Safety and Health, the European Agency for Safety and Health at Work, and the European Commission published by The American Institute of Stress, a professional organization dedicated to effective stress management.

- Forty percent of workers said that their job is very or extremely stressful.
- Twenty five percent said that the number-one stressor in their lives is their job
- Job stress is strongly associated with health complaints, more than family or financial problems.
- Eighty percent of workers report feeling stress on the job, and nearly one-half say that they need help in learning how to manage their stress.

- Twenty nine percent had yelled at coworkers because of stress at work.

- The following physical maladies were reported due to stress in a 2000 study: neck pain (62 percent), stressed-out eyes (44 percent), hurting hands (38 percent), and difficulty sleeping (34 percent).

- Job stress costs U.S. industry more than $300 billion per year.

- Approximately 1 million workers are absent from the workplace every day due to stress.

(American Institute of Stress, 2003)

More important than money, the personal cost to stressed-out workers is sobering: depression, anxiety, anger, substance abuse, heart disease, and frequent headaches. Because both physical and emotional well-being is affected, stress has an important effect on employees' professional and personal lives.

In correctional institutions, this is serious. Cheek (1984) cited studies in New York and California that found that correctional personnel used more sick leave than other state workers. California spent almost $2 million in overtime costs to cover one-half of correctional workers who were on sick leave in 1975-76. Today, correctional administrators are faced with tight budgets and increasing costs. Research indicates that correctional officers tend to use more sick leave than those in other staff positions (Lovrich et al., 1990). While recent trends in corrections and stress will be further discussed in Chapter 3, one can assume that many of the problems listed above are present in correctional environments, combined with agency monetary shortfalls, crowded facilities, short staffing, more violent inmates, and so on.

An example that illustrates the problem of stress and corrections is California, with one of the largest departments of corrections in the United States with thirty-one prisons (American Correctional Association, 2004). In 2001, the California Department of Corrections "busted" its budget with overuse of correctional officer sick leave and overtime. Correctional staff used 2.3 million hours of sick leave, which was 64 percent over what had been planned for in the agency budget. To cover the officers out sick, the California Department of Corrections paid $87 million in overtime, creating a huge budget shortfall. A California Department of Corrections spokesman said that the use of sick leave is understandable, considering the conditions that correctional officers face at work. "We have people being injured and people more susceptible to illnesses created by or exacerbated by stress."

A spokesman for the California Correctional Peace Officer's Association said that the use of sick leave is legitimate. He also said that "the stress is unrelenting....The fact that employees use a benefit that's awarded to them, and that's a negative issue, I fail to understand...[auditors should] take off their pocket protectors and find out what it is like to work in a prison where correctional officers are forced to work double shifts and routinely confront dangers such as violence and communicable diseases." He added that corrections is "a very demoralizing job" (Hill, 2001).

Of course, this is one correctional agency, but there are others including jails that suffer staff shortages and have no funds to hire new staff, the probation and parole officers who watch as their caseloads go up and staffing goes down or remains stationary.

Defining Stress

After hearing the word "stress" over and over, many people think they know what it means (Whittlesey 1986). The problem is that most people have misconceptions about stress.

A homemaker may perceive stress as unending housework, too many loads of laundry, grocery shopping with high food costs, appliances breaking, and dealing with sick children. To construction workers, stress might mean inclement weather for their working conditions, tools breaking, and late deliveries of construction supplies. Teachers might define stress as unruly children, conflicting demands from the school board, or a lack of textbooks. People experience stress in a variety of other situations, from working in the yard to paying bills, from worrying about the health of a loved one, to worrying about being overweight, from reprimands from the boss to arguments with their spouse.

Although people's perceptions of stress indicate they understand that stress is part of everyday life, most people mistake the stressor for the stress. According to Dr. Hans Selye (1907-1982), a pioneer in stress research, a stressor is something that "produces stress." It is the event, person, or circumstance that triggers a physical and mental reaction (Selye, 1974).

Selye defined stress as the "nonspecific response of the body to any demand made upon it." Selye says that each demand made on us is specific—a new job, marriage, a new assignment, an argument—but the response, which is nonspecific, forces us to adapt, whether the demand is good or bad (Selye, 1974). However, another definition of stress is that "Stress is tension or pressures that are a natural part of living our lives. Changes and events in our lives (getting married, illness, changing jobs) are a major source of stress," according to the Psychiatric Institute of Washington, D.C. (1985).

According to Selye, stress cannot be avoided. Because stress is a part of everyday life, we must constantly respond and adapt to all types of changes every day. How we deal with these demands can affect our health directly.

"Just Being Sick"

Selye discovered that common characteristics of patients suffering from injuries, cancer, and infectious diseases included weight loss, apathy, lack of appetite, and weakness, or a general lack of energy. He called this syndrome "just being sick." Selye discovered that other conditions as well as illness and disease, could cause a person to have the "just-being-sick" syndrome. As a result, his research led him to conclude that when people undergo changes—whether good or bad, no matter if the changes are emotional or physical—their bodies also go through changes (Whittlesey, 1986).

More important, these changes often go unnoticed. If these internal changes continue and our health is not good, over time, a "weak link" in our bodies will break down and fail. For example, Joe has not watched his weight in ten years, nor has he had a medical check up or a cardiovascular stress test. His company has just restructured, doubling Joe's workload. Joe must handle more meetings, more tasks, and more problems than before. After six months of working under this pressure, Joe suffers a serious heart attack. In this example, the changes were in Joe's workload and the weak link was his heart, which gave out.

Positive and negative stressors are part of our everyday lives, both on and off the job. Whether the stressors are good, such as going on vacation, getting married, receiving visitors, or buying new furniture, or bad, such as experiencing a death in the family, tending to sick children, or having to fix leaky plumbing, they produce a reaction—stress.

Negative Stressors

Correctional staff, including security officers, juvenile care workers, doctors and nurses, teachers, and probation officers, encounter a gamut of possible stressors, ranging from inmate fights, bad odors, offenders missing appointments, noisy cellblocks, offender grievances, disciplinary hearings, inmate attacks on officers, increased caseloads, unending paperwork, argumentative attorneys, suicide victims, offenders under the influence of drugs or alcohol, court appearances, and inmate lawsuits. As we will see in Chapter 3, there are many stressors in correctional work.

The stressor and stress should not be confused with each other—they are not interchangeable. For example, having to appear in court is not stress; it is a stressor—

it causes us to react. Faced with a court appearance, a correctional officer or parole officer may feel nervous, "up tight," or anxious. Those feelings are the reactions (stress) caused by the stressor (having to go to court).

Positive Stressors

Some stressors can be positive and produce favorable reactions. Stressors in this category include receiving a letter of appreciation from a supervisor, having an inmate thank you for being helpful, learning that a parolee successfully completed parole, finding a job for a work-release inmate, or successfully intervening to help an inmate in crisis. Positive stressors also include exercise, a pleasant change to a routine (such as answering the door and having an old friend standing there) or intimate relations and sex. The changes produced and the reactions are pleasurable and pleasant.

For example, if you receive a telephone call from an inmate's father thanking you for helping his son get enrolled in a drug program, you feel good, you smile, and your self-esteem goes up. These are positive reactions.

Stress Reactions: Body and Mind

Pressures and tensions from life result in good and bad changes that trigger our stress alarms (Psychiatric Institute of Washington, D.C., 1985). When we are confronted with stressors, our minds and bodies react and get ready to adapt to the stressor. Selye believes that adapting to stress requires "adaptive energy." This energy is crucial in stress management. According to Selye, adaptive energy comes in two forms: a "local resource" that is used in normal everyday life, and a second type that is held in reserve for emergencies (Cheek, 1984). For example, people use adaptive energy constantly—responding to the changes and demands placed on us. It is the "reserve" adaptive energy—the energy we need to meet stressors, such as inmate arguments or assaults—that is crucial to successfully managing stress. Stress reaction or the adaptive process occurs in three stages: alarm or arousal, resistance, and exhaustion (Cheek 1984).

The Alarm Stage

The alarm or immediate stage (Adler, Kalb and Rogers, 1999) marks the first contact with the stressor. Things start to happen. The hypothalamus, the part of the brain that controls basic drives and emotions, signals the adrenal and pituitary glands to "beware" or "get ready." These signals trigger the "fight-or-flight reaction" (Whittlesey, 1986).

The fight-or-flight reaction prepares us to meet the stressor head on (fight) or to run from it (flight). Whatever happens, the body is ready. Whatever the stressor—good or bad—the body is mobilized.

During the alarm stage, the body undergoes more than 1,400 physical changes due to the adrenal gland secreting adrenalin and other substances. These physical changes include the following (Cheek, 1984; Adler, Kalb and Rogers, 1999):

- increased heart rate, your blood pressure goes up
- blood pumps faster, directed now to muscles, which tense
- the liver converts sugar stored as glycogen to glucose
- extra red blood cells carrying vital oxygen flow from the spleen; fats and sugars are released in the bloodstream for an energy boost for power
- the ability to clot blood increases
- pupils of eyes dilate, improving vision
- respiration increases as the lungs take in more oxygen
- perspiration (sweating) increases
- digestion halts, which allows more energy to be shifted to the muscles
- the brain dulls the body's sense of pain
- thinking and memory improve
- adrenaline—the fight-or-flight hormone epinephrine—is secreted
- body hair becomes more erect; this evolved from animals looking bigger and more dangerous

Once the body is ready, the decision must be made to meet the stressor or run. In corrections, most duties as well as moral and legal obligations dictate that workers meet the stressor and not flee. However, this may not be true in all cases. For example, a probation officer receives a call from the receptionist indicating that one of her clients is waiting to see her and is obviously angry. She sees the client (fight reaction)—she does not ask the receptionist to make up an excuse as she sneaks out the back door (flight). A jail officer looks into a cellblock and sees two inmates fighting. The initial reaction may be to fight—go in and break it up. But he thinks, "I'm alone. It could be a set up. I'd better get back up." He backs off (flight) to notify other officers, then with help on the way, goes in (fight) and breaks it up. The corrections profession is unique in this way—a variety of problems call for a variety of reactions. Most of the time, however, correctional workers must meet head on whatever comes their way.

The Resistance Stage

The second stage of stress reaction then sets in. This is the resistance or adaptation stage. Some researchers call it the delayed stage (Adler, Kalb, and Rogers, 1999) where the body stabilizes and replenishes itself. If the stressful situation continues, the body continues the changes that started in the first stage. The heart still pumps faster, perspiration continues, and so on. According to Adler, Kalb, and Rogers (1999), the body undergoes the following processes:

- in the brain, the center of memory and learning (the hippocampus) activates to process the stress
- the immune system decreases activity to increase available energy
- the liver converts fat into usable fuel
- cortisol, sometimes called "The Stress Hormone," is secreted by the adrenal glands to regulate the body's metabolism and blood pressure. The secretion of this vital hormone increases during the body's response to any kind of physical and psychological stress (Stoppler, 2004).

For example, a correctional officer steps between two inmates who are insulting each other. The officer goes through the alarm stage—his body tenses up; he is ready to respond if the situation escalates into a fight. The situation continues and the insults are getting louder and uglier. The officer is now in the adaptive stage. His body is still adapting—this will continue as long as the stressor (argument) continues.

In the adaptive stage, his overall health and physical condition are important. In the previous example, the officer's heart must be able to sustain a rapid heartbeat and his lungs must be able to continue breathing rapidly. In other words, his body must outlast the stressor. If it cannot, the officer may suffer a heart attack, run out of breath, collapse, or just "run out of steam."

Adaptive energy is like a savings account in a bank. When one needs money in an emergency, money is withdrawn to meet the need. It is the same with adaptive energy. It must be available when it is needed during stressful situations to help the body meet the stressor.

Once the stressful situation is over, the body returns to a pre-alarm state. In other words, we calm down. After a fight or after an unruly inmate is restrained, officers tend to talk a lot, relax, joke around, and unwind. They are returning to the pre-alarm state until the next time a stressor is encountered, and the alarm stage starts the cycle all over again.

The Exhaustion Stage

The third stage of stress reaction is called the exhaustion stage, although this stage does not necessarily have to be reached. When the body cannot resist the stressor any longer, exhaustion occurs. Vulnerability to illness and physical ailments and behavioral problems, such as anger or depression, can set in. The body simply gives out (Whittlesey, 1986). Sometimes called the "chronic stage," the body undergoes these changes (Adler, Kalb, and Rogers, 1999):

- If the stress response is activated too often (as it often is in corrections), the immune system, the brain, and the heart may be harmed.

- The cortisol that is secreted during the resistance stage may become toxic to brain cells. Cognitive ability may be damaged. Fatigue, depression, and anger increase.

- Due to the repeated suppression of disease-fighting cells in the resistance stage, resistance to infection is weakened.

- The mucous lining of the intestines may become vulnerable to ulcers because of decreased blood flow.

- The elasticity of the blood vessels is damaged due to an elevated heart rate and increased blood pressure.

For example, the heart can give out after years of dealing with offenders in stressful situations. Heart disease and high blood pressure can develop if the correctional worker rides a roller coaster of the alarm-adaptation-calm cycle for years. If the worker smokes, never exercises, and does little or nothing to promote cardiovascular fitness, the worker may be more prone than his or her coworkers to reach the exhaustion stage, where a heart attack could result.

It is important to remember that if we successfully adapt to stress and work to keep healthy in body and mind, we may never reach the exhaustion stage. If we do reach this stage from time to time, a healthy lifestyle and good coping practices can serve to get us out of exhaustion quickly. Some stress researchers compare this concept to the experience of athletes. Training for long-distance running or swimming may be stressful, and the athlete may reach physical exhaustion. In time, however, the athlete's body adapts to the exercise and it takes longer to reach exhaustion (Whittlesey, 1986). One of the most important goals in managing stress is to be mentally and physically healthy enough so as not to fall into the exhaustion stage.

Short-Term Stress versus Long-Term Stress

Stress can be divided into two categories: short-term and long-term. Short-term, or healthy stress, is stress that does not last long and can be handled easily. Examples of this type of stress are exercise, such as running one mile per day, meeting a new boss, starting work in the jail just after graduating from the academy, and writing your first presentence report.

On the other hand, long-term stress is stress that eventually can cause trouble if it is not managed properly. In corrections, long-term stress can take many forms, such as crowded conditions, heavy caseloads, numerous regulations, paperwork, and inmates or clients who constantly demand attention. Long-term stress forces correctional workers to move between the first two reaction stages—alarm and adaptation—and never relax. This can continue for a long time until the correctional worker reaches exhaustion.

There are many examples of the effects of long-term stress. Officers who find it hard to relax often complain of stomach problems or headaches. Parole officers who become "workaholics" over the years often wind up with high blood pressure. Not managing long-term stress takes a toll both physically and mentally.

Mentally, workers who never "ease up" may experience physical and behavioral symptoms as the effects of long-term stress continue. The worker's body and mind begin to wear down as the stress continues. Stress can even affect the body's immune system, causing increased vulnerability to colds, flu, and other ailments.

Physical and Behavioral Signs of Stress

Your body usually tells you when you are not effectively managing your stress by giving warning signs, such as skin disorders; head-, neck-, or backaches; an upset stomach or nausea; dizziness; ulcers; insomnia; heart disease; cold hands or feet; high blood pressure; irregular bowel movements; a rapid pulse; teeth grinding; a clenched jaw; shortness of breath; trembling/shaking; weight gain/loss; and problems in sexual relations (Cornelius, 1991; Harper, 1992; Kiffer, 2002).

The body will break down due to the wear and tear of stress. A jail counselor who works two straight weeks with no time off due to staff shortages may start to feel queasy. A juvenile counselor who has not taken a vacation in three years may begin having problems sleeping.

Stress has behavioral affects, too. Like physical symptoms, certain warning signs in workers' personalities, behaviors, and dealings with others start to show. These

From calm to a serious incident: the unexpected is inherent in corrections work.

signals include negativity toward inmates or clients; difficulty relaxing; anger or irritability; eating disorders; anxiety; boredom; impatience; an increased use of drugs, alcohol, tobacco, or caffeine; indecision; and frequent accidents or mistakes.

Stressed-out correctional workers may be impatient, not only with inmates and clients, but also with family, friends, and coworkers. They may angrily overreact to minor problems, tasks, or situations they formerly took in stride. Some workers become bored and apathetic about their jobs and life in general. They may drag themselves home and then "veg out" in front of the television. Workers who smoke may increase the number of cigarettes they smoke. Workers may start drinking alcoholic beverages more often to relax. They may start abusing drugs to escape the stress. They may be increasingly tense and anxious as they drive to work, succumbing to "road rage."

Depression can set in as moodiness, apathy, lack of hygiene, and self-destructive thoughts. Officers may not call for a backup when entering a dangerous situation or inmate area. They may become "adventurous" where before prudent behavior and training said not to be. Mood swings in minutes or hours are a sign. Another is change in personality. Colleagues may point out that "Officer ___ is not himself" or "Why is he acting that way?" The stressed person's attitude may be "Get away—I don't need any help" (National Association of Chiefs of Police, 1995).

Stress Effects Us

Stress, if not managed properly, can have a definite effect on how correctional personnel feel physically and also on how they behave toward themselves and others. Stressed-out correctional workers are "stress carriers"—they feel the physical and behavioral effects constantly and their behavior can strain their professional and personal lives.

Over a twenty-to-thirty year career, and in daily life, a correctional worker—in no matter what area, takes the proverbial roller coaster ride, up one hill and down the other. The hills on the ride are crises that bring on the stress reaction. The valleys represent coming down, relaxing, and recharging adaptive energy before the next crisis hits. If we exhaust ourselves, we go off the track. This is the stress cycle. It is a part of life.

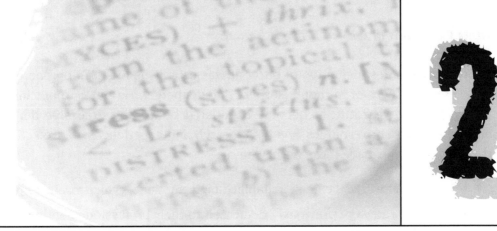

Burnout

After reading this chapter, you should understand the following:

- What "burnout" is
- How to identify the signs of burnout
- The five stages of burnout
- How burnout affects you, your family, your friends, and coworkers
- How to avoid burnout

Burnout is one aspect of stress management. Part of managing stress effectively and living a positive lifestyle is avoiding the burnout stage. Unfortunately, correctional workers frequently ignore the signs of stress and burnout. In the roll-call rooms or in the probation office, staff hear their colleagues say that they are "burned out," or that someone left the field because he or she was "burned out."

Burnout has several different definitions. One view is that burnout "refers to a debilitating psychological condition brought about by unrelieved work stress" (Veninga and Spradley, 1981). Another view is that burnout is "a state of physical, emotional, and mental exhaustion caused by long-term involvement in situations that are emotionally demanding" (Hill, 1991). Some researchers attribute burnout to "stress [that] has been so intense for such a long period that it is difficult for an employee to perform even the most basic requirements of his [or] her job" (Morris, 1986). Some researchers describe the state of being burned out as "severe emotional fatigue, resulting in negative attitudes and feelings by correctional officers toward both officers (or coworkers) and inmates (or clients)" (Kauffman, 1988).

Probably the best definition of burnout was established in 1974 by one of the pioneering researchers of burnout, Herbert Freudenberger. He put burnout into simple terms: "to fail, wear out, or become exhausted by making excessive demands on energy, strength, or resources." As his research and experience as a free clinic director progressed, he made these observations:

- Burned-out workers exhibit irritability, high emotions, cynicism, and depression.

- Workers who were previously dedicated to their profession spend more time at work, but accomplish less.

- Boredom sets in with the routine of dealing with clients and their problems in a repetitious manner.

- Burnout is related to the loss of one's ideals and is similar to a grief experience followed almost always by anger.

- Burnout is a chronic condition of fatigue and/or frustration caused by a devotion to a cause, an ideal, a way of life, or relationship that did not produce the expected reward.

- Exhaustion can result from excessive demands in a human-service occupation by workers trying to reach unrealistic expectations imposed by society or the workers themselves

  (Freudenberger, 1974 and 1980; Whitehead, 1989).

These definitions contain several key elements: unrelieved work stress; long-term involvement in demanding situations; continuous, intense stress; irritability; exhaustion; cynicism; depression; boredom; loss of ideals; anger; frustration; and fatigue. People who are burned out have not learned to effectively manage stress by relaxing or positively coping with stressors. Stressors—perceived mostly as bad—and the reactions they cause, are on their minds all the time. Exhaustion sets in, and they never get back to the pre-alarm stage.

Translate this information to the field of corrections. Many of us in corrections came into the field with high ideals—we wanted to "make a difference" and help people. As the demands of life and the stressful occupation take their toll, frustrated correctional staff start to run out of steam in a cynical, frustrated way.

Burnout: A History

The term "burnout" has a colorful history. One way to understand the concept of burnout is to think of stress as combat—you are the soldier fighting the enemy over a long period of time.

During the Civil War, soldiers who collapsed were believed to be insane because they were suffering from "paralysis." During World War I, soldiers who became severely fatigued were diagnosed as having "shell shock." During World War II, military psychiatrists did not support the "shell shock" diagnosis. Instead, doctors believed that soldiers who collapsed under battle conditions suffered from "combat psychoneurosis."

Once it was recognized that constant battle conditions and combat can cause battle stress, the military developed ways to minimize the effects of what was officially called "combat fatigue." During the Vietnam War, soldiers received frequent "rest and relaxation" periods away from the war zone. Also, tours of duty were limited to no more than thirteen months. As a result, the number of combat-fatigue cases showed a marked decrease (Veninga and Spradley, 1981).

Burnout is complicated by the fact that many people have misconceptions about it. Sometimes, diagnosing burnout is easy: correctional officers who are constantly angry and seem to lose control easily and formerly dedicated probation officers who say they "don't give a damn" anymore are burned out. Offenders often are the first to recognize the signs of burnout in a correctional worker. For example, they notice when a custodial officer, who used to walk through housing units checking on inmates, now avoids talking with them.

Identifying Burnout

Frequently, signs of burnout are not recognized. For example, a sergeant sees that one of the officers in his squad is always tired. A secretary in the jail hears a file clerk say that the filing will "take care of itself." A good worker becomes a chronic complainer where nothing is good about the facility, the staff, or the inmates. These workers may be suffering from burnout—the fatigue and lazy attitude are probably just symptoms of the underlying problem.

Often, when correctional workers look at their colleagues who exhibit these symptoms, they blame the behavior on the symptoms, "the sarge is snapping at us because he's really tired," or "Cindy has an upset stomach often—that's why she's not up to par." It is easy to label someone as lazy or bored because they are not producing. The laziness may be the result of exhaustion.

The following behaviors are common in burned-out employees:

- exhaustion
- apathy or lack of involvement with the job

- inability to relax

- bitterness or sour attitude

- low morale

- constant complaining about the job or working conditions

- frequent impatience or easily frustrated

- always tense

- frequently calls in sick or leaves work for slightest reason

- lack of interaction with coworkers

Workers who are burned out have let the stress build up over time. It is important to recognize that there is no set time limit or period in which workers burn out. It can happen sooner for some than for others. This explains why some correctional officers become angry and bitter after only a year or two on the job, while others can work fifteen years before becoming burned out.

Why do some correctional workers burn out and others do not? Everyone has an individual way of dealing (or not dealing) with stress. How fast a correctional worker burns out depends on how that person perceives the stress surrounding him or her.

According to Robert Veninga and James Spradley, authors of *The Work Stress Connection: How to Cope with Job Burnout*, people are more apt to burn out if they view stress negatively. People heading for burnout view stressors as "disasters" or hassles. For example, Gregg, a probation officer, has just been assigned a caseload of the ten most serious offenders his department supervises. These offenders do not have good records and have caused other probation officers problems. Gregg looks on the new assignment as one more hassle he does not need and silently asks, "Why me? Why not someone else?" He feels taken advantage of and is openly angry. He feels that he is getting a "raw deal."

Gregg, like most burnouts, will complain to his supervisor, coworkers, family, and friends. His complaints will be continuous and loud. Eventually, family, friends, and coworkers will tire of Gregg's constant griping, and may shy away and avoid him. When they do, the negative feelings Gregg is experiencing will get worse—he will think, "no one listens" or "no one cares." A very important support mechanism is gone. In Gregg's case, he will exhaust himself by complaining and looking at the assignment in a negative way.

On the other hand, in another probation office, Probation Officer Joanne gets a similar assignment. Joanne is not yet at the burnout stage. She views this assignment realistically—it is more stress, but it is also a challenge. Part of Joanne's positive attitude is that this is an opportunity to increase her client-management skills. Joanne begins by studying available materials on the types of offenders she will be supervising as a way to increase the possibility of her success. Her chances for promotion may increase because of this assignment, and Joanne knows it. This is an example of good stress.

There is a big difference between Gregg and Joanne. Gregg will look at the stress as negative, which will exhaust him at a faster rate. Joanne, on the other hand, may not burn out at all.

There are other factors that may cause a correctional worker to burn out faster. They include the following:

- ineffective or no support network
- negative surroundings
- lack of or ineffective stress-coping techniques

The Five Stages of Burnout

Burnout does not happen overnight. It develops through stages, each with certain behaviors and warning signs. Veninga and Spradley (1981) list these progressive stages of burnout:

- honeymoon
- fuel shortage
- chronic symptoms
- crisis
- "hitting the wall"

These stages progress from the least severe to the most critical. Many correctional workers go up to the fourth stage, but never reach the final stage.

Honeymoon

Correctional workers in the honeymoon stage have a strong sense of enthusiasm, exhibit a lot of energy, and have a strong desire to do well. They are very excited about their jobs. For example, George is a deputy sheriff who has worked the cellblocks at the county jail for five years. Even though he likes corrections, George wishes to get out of the custody section and be a jail-classification officer. The shifts, noise, and tension of the cellblocks are beginning to take their toll. George feels tired and frustrated.

George is promoted to corporal and is assigned to the jail-classification unit. He is excited, full of enthusiasm, and impresses his superiors as a "hard charger"—an officer who will carry more than his share of the load. George puts in extra time, skips lunches, and is constantly on the go. He enjoys conducting intake interviews on inmates and counseling them about their problems. He sees his role at the facility as challenging and worthwhile. George views stress as part of the territory—it is exciting to "be on the go." To him, at this time, stress is energizing.

George is in the "honeymoon stage." He loves his job, both the good and all the bad. He is a "hard charger." George is not unusual. No matter what area of work, people often are "hard chargers" when they start their careers or new assignments.

"Honeymooners" in this stage are using up their adaptive energy. Their energies are poured into their jobs. Because they perceive stressors as challenging, they do not give much thought to managing stress. George does not worry about a balanced diet and regularly has a bag of chips and a soda for a quick lunch. George often works double shifts and volunteers to work on his days off. It is unusual for him to sleep more than five or six hours a night. With all the work and other demands on his time, he believes he has no time left in his day for exercise. But what George does not realize is that this lifestyle, which revolves around his work, has a price he will be forced to pay later.

Fuel Shortage

At this stage, the "hard-charging" worker begins to slow down a bit. According to Veninga and Spradley (1981), workers may feel a loss or think that their jobs have not lived up to their expectations. Correctional workers may feel disillusioned with their job and may find it more difficult to be satisfied in it. Their work may suffer. They may feel depressed because they are always tired, in stark contrast to the "honeymoon" period when being tired did not bother them. Workers in this stage may find it hard to fall asleep or need to sleep more than usual.

This is also the stage when workers usually begin developing negative-coping techniques in an attempt to escape from too much tension and strain. Overeating, increased smoking, shopping sprees, and excess drinking are just some of the signs indicating a worker has reached this stage. Workers' physical and mental health start to suffer, causing the adaptive energy or fuel needed to deal with stress to run out.

One day, George, the classification officer, realizes he no longer enjoys going to the jail every day. Working double shifts and conducting record numbers of intake interviews have lost their luster. What was once a challenge to help inmates and "make a difference" is turning into drudgery. George gets tired more and more easily. When he goes home, he sits and mindlessly watches whatever is on television. The honeymoon is over.

Chronic Symptoms

At this stage, workers feel that something serious may be physically wrong with them, and they may see their doctor as a result. One thing is now certain—the signs of stress cannot be easily ignored.

Along with an overall exhaustion, workers also experience a variety of physical ailments, such as constipation, diarrhea, stomach disorders, skin rashes, headaches, backaches, and nausea. The constant "sick feeling" adds to a worker's anger, irritability, and impatience. Where minor problems were handled quickly and without much difficulty, workers now may blow things out of proportion. This happens at home, too. A child's messy room or simple errands after work become major irritants. And without much provocation, workers snap at their spouse or lash out at family members. Workers in this stage usually direct a lot of anger toward their job and express it with comments such as "it stinks" and "I hate it." The anger affects coworkers, who note the "short fuse" and try as much as possible to give burned-out employees a wide berth.

Two things may happen to correctional workers in this stage. First, family members, friends, coworkers, and inmates or clients will notice the changes taking place. Workers suffering from burnout become "stress carriers" (Cheek, 1984). For example, a parole officer gripes so much about his job that no one in the office wants to be near him. At home, he is withdrawn and tunes the family out. Becoming irritable over small things, the burned-out parole officer gives less and less emotional support to his family. He becomes cold (Cheek, 1984). Fights, arguments, and squabbles start in his family. Then, the officer begins feeling as if he is caught in a vise, because now the stress is everywhere—both at work and at home. Instead of allowing his family to help him, the parole officer's strong, tough-guy image at work creates barriers in his home life, too. When suppressed emotions become too much to keep in, outbursts of anger, targeted at family, friends, colleagues, and inmates or clients, result (Cheek, 1984).

Depression is common in workers at this level of burnout, according to Veninga and Spradley (1981). Their research indicates that although unrelieved stress is not the only cause, decreasing or nonexistent energy reserves, pressures at work and at home, and problems due to burnout can lead to depression.

George, the classification officer, realizes now that the job is not meeting his initial expectations. He suffers from chronic headaches, and he tunes out his family by watching a lot of television. He does not say much about work, except to bitterly complain about some new problem. His wife and children start to avoid him, not wanting to be the target of his irritable snaps and angry outbursts.

Crisis

At this critical stage of burnout, physical symptoms, such as high blood pressure, stomach problems, muscle aches, and headaches, get worse. As work efficiency begins to decrease, workers start doubting their ability to do a good job. Correctional workers in this stage are obsessed by the job and their frustrations with it. It seems as if these thoughts are with the worker every waking moment—thoughts like the job "stinks," "no one cares," and "I've had enough." In this frame of mind, it is difficult to enjoy other aspects of life, such as family outings, movies, and social gatherings.

Escape activities begun earlier are worse now. "Relaxation sessions" with other officers at a bar after work get longer. Thoughts of quitting, even without another job lined up, are prominent. Time until retirement is calculated to the day.

George's daily headaches are beginning to wear him down. He is overeating. His supervisor indicates during a performance evaluation that George's complaining has lowered the morale of coworkers in the unit. Angry outbursts at home and work continue. As George walks into the jail at the beginning of each shift, all he can think about is the "crap" that is his job. He is sick of inmates, their problems, and the paperwork. As he thinks these thoughts, his stomach tightens up and his heart beats faster. He is sweating, knowing that he has a full day ahead in a job he hates. George's physical and mental problems are getting the best of him before he even starts work.

As a correctional officer, George's poor job efficiency and negative feelings toward his job and the inmates may cause him to not notice a suicidal inmate or to overlook critical information other jail staff need to know.

"Hitting the Wall"

This is the last stage of burnout—the stage where everything falls apart. The body no longer can endure the stress. The adaptive energy is gone. Mentally, the workers no longer can function. Veninga and Spradley state that by the time a worker "hits the wall," the ailments he has been suffering are intertwined with burnout: substance abuse, mental disorders (such as depression), and heart problems.

Some workers at this level of burnout may snap. Quitting the job abruptly or walking out on the family is not uncommon for workers in this stage. Others may commit senseless acts of anger and violence, such as hitting someone or throwing things.

George has gotten worse. He knows that job stress is getting to him. He promises his wife that he will fix some things around the house and try to relax during his next day off. But recently, he has worked several sixteen-hour days. And for the past two days, all he could think about is the job—how bad it is, how he is sick of it, and how nothing ever gets better.

On his day off, George gets out his tools and the new deadbolt lock he promised his wife he would install on the front door. After taking the old deadbolt off the wooden front door, George begins to put on the new one. He cannot get the lock lined up properly on the doorframe. The wood is old and splintering. Suddenly, George is very angry. He thinks this is just one more hassle in a long line of hassles—the job, the inmates, and the staff that shy away from him. He feels himself boiling, and still the lock will not line up. Losing control, George blows his top and punches a hole in the wall.

Can George or correctional workers like him be helped? Can they reverse the stages of burnout?

Some workers never reach the last stage because they recognize the signs that stress is ravaging their physical and mental health, and they take steps to positively cope with the stress. Others must reach the hitting-the-wall stage before they can step back and realize they must do something about the stress they feel. The good thing is that there is something George, and others like him, can do to reverse burnout. They can learn to manage their stress. Realizing that change is necessary is an important first step.

Effect on Family and Friends

Job burnout has been called an impairment of motivation to work. A burnout acts withdrawn, looks as if he or she is bored, and the quality of his or her work declines. Additionally, it has been called an "inability to mobilize enough interest to act." Prevention of burnout means maintaining motivation (Pranzo and Pranzo, 1999).

How does that translate into relations with family, friends, and coworkers? In family relations, including marriage, the burnout has no motivation to build or keep a positive relationship maintained. The kids and the wife may want to go somewhere, the "burnout" husband and daddy wants to be left alone. Griping and being cynical increase to the point where the family or significant other does not want to be around the burnout. Emotional outbursts, arguments, separation, and divorce may result. Another result may be extramarital affairs where the burnout looks for solace, support, and an answer to boredom by engaging in infidelity.

It is similar with friends. It is important to have friends outside of the corrections profession. It gives us a refreshed point of view, where we are interested in others—their opinions, their jobs, and so forth. "If you maintain a wide circle of friends who are not in corrections, you will have sounding boards and can hear what is being said by other people with other perspectives on what we do in our profession" (Bartollas, 2004, p. 89). However, if the family members and significant others of a burnout find themselves avoiding the burnout or arguing with him or her, then friendships will suffer. Social engagements, fun, and activities will fall off as people realize that "hanging around with so and so" means listening to him gripe about his job all evening.

Finally, let us talk about coworkers. Burnouts on the job may act like an anchor tossed into a leaky lifeboat—burnouts can drag all of us down. We in corrections depend on each other—inside correctional facilities, in the probation/parole offices, and in the juvenile centers. We watch out for each other. We have to cooperate—no matter what the agency—to get the job done. Burnouts are difficult people with whom to work. Burnouts may be bored and miss contraband on a search. Burnouts may be so cynical that they verbally "push the buttons" of an inmate and a fight results. Burnouts withdraw as they begin to realize that they are disliked and no one wants to work with them. Burnouts quietly sit in a corner during roll calls or staff meetings, away from others, and do not engage in dialog with colleagues. They arrive late for work or do not show up at all by calling in sick (Monta, 2002). The end results are alienated coworkers, a weak spot in the security network, and a downward turn of morale.

In all three groups—family/significant others, friends, and colleagues—the physical ailments of burnout: minor colds, headaches, backaches, insomnia, being jittery/tense, and the "tired or rundown" feelings will have a negative affect. So do the negative coping techniques of abusing alcohol or drugs, eating disorders, smoking, and increased drinking of coffee (Pranzo and Pranzo, 1999). If you are behaviorally a mess, and physically a mess, you cannot fully get along with others—on and off the job.

Avoiding Burnout: Building an Effective Support Network

An effective support network includes friends, both on and off the job, and can be crucial in effectively managing stress. Friends and family are important because they can help reason through a situation and can build the self-esteem of a burned-out worker. They also help a worker focus on other aspects of his or her life, and thus relax. Close friends and loved ones can help stressed-out people in times of need. They can listen and offer support and advice. Often, the first thing someone does after a bad day at work is to call a friend and talk about the day's events. Another way to look at this is to have the burnouts talk frequently about what bothers them with "safe people." Safe people are those people with whom the burnouts can get their problems out of their system and are a "buffer" against burnout and stress (Pranzo and Pranzo, 1999).

As a twenty-year continuous study of 7,000 people in Alameda County, California, discovered, people who did not have any close emotional bonds to family or friends had a two- to five-times higher rate of death than people who did have important, sustaining, and healthy interpersonal relationships. Interacting with friends and family is healthy—and can keep a worker interested in positive coping techniques, such as healthy eating, exercising, and relaxing (Whittlesey, 1986).

Unfortunately, many burned-out workers do not have effective support networks. Sometimes the lack of a support network is self-inflicted, because burnouts tend to alienate their friends and family, causing them to distance themselves. For example, Maria, a counselor at a county juvenile facility, was burned out after just two years on the job. She constantly complained about her job to her husband, which made him feel alienated. The new distance in their relationship made both of them tense and resulted in more frequent arguments—adding not only to Maria's stress but contributing to her husband's as well.

Avoiding Burnout: Transforming Negative Surroundings

Both the work and home environment can affect the amount of stress correctional professionals experience. For example, a probation officer who is near burnout is under even more stress when her desk is moved into a small, windowless cubicle, and an exhausted jail secretary comes home to a cluttered apartment and feels like giving up. In a busy lifestyle, messy, cluttered, and unorganized homes and workplaces can add to the list of stressors.

Although a messy desk can be organized and a cluttered office cleaned out, some things in the environment cannot be changed as easily. Traffic jams, the weather, and the age and condition of the jail or office building are all out of an individual's control. Corrections professionals have to learn when to accept certain stressors as a part of life. Although a building may be old, it can be freshly painted. And although a probation officer may not be able to avoid the move into a small office, it can be decorated and kept uncluttered. Many people, in fact, underestimate the benefits of keeping their homes cleaned up and comfortably decorated to serve as a refuge after a harrowing day.

Avoiding Burnout: Learning Stress-Coping Techniques

People who are burned-out cope negatively with stress. Many abuse alcohol or drugs to "numb" themselves against stress or to relax. Others overeat or chain smoke. Often, the exhaustion caused by burnout results in loss of interest in health and exercise. Generally, mental and physical health decline as these harmful practices continue. Adaptive energy decreases.

Workers who resist burnout cope positively (*see* Chapter 4). They exercise, do not smoke, watch their diets, and drink alcohol in moderation. They take care of themselves and maintain their reserve of adaptive energy. They make it a point to engage in stress-management techniques, knowing that if they do not, they can fall victim to the exhaustion stage and burnout.

Avoiding Burnout: Letting Go

One coping technique of stress management is the ability to let things go. Burnouts have a way of fixating on things—"the captain is a jerk, this job is hell," and so forth. Letting things go means to accept things that you are powerless to change and not to get overly stressed out over them.

Letting go also means that a job or career change or transfer may be necessary. There is nothing wrong with considering a career change if corrections is making you unhappy. Maybe you have tried all sorts of stress-coping strategies, and have discovered that you would be happier in another line of work. You—yourself—are priority one. Talk it over with your significant other or family. Weigh the options. Is a job change what you need?

Letting go also means taking time off. Many of us say in corrections: "Yeah, right. The captain will never let me take leave." Have you asked? Or, is it better to just give up and stew about it? Maybe you should work with your supervisor, and split up your time off instead of taking one big "chunk" of time all at once. This will lessen the impact on the staff and show your supervisor that you are considerate of others on the staff.

As one veteran correctional worker observes:

I never used to take much time off, maybe a week total in the summer. I was earning more annual leave per pay period and as I grew older and put more time on the job, I began to realize that leave would be better used for family outings and more weeks of vacation per year than sitting on the books. So, I began to take more time off, especially when I felt stressed out or more importantly, burned out. Taking time off served to recharge my batteries.

Getting a grip on burnout simply means to get a grip on managing your stress. Whatever workers can do on and off the job to manage stress—turn them away from the exhaustion stage—and as a result, avoid burnout, they should do.

Corrections: A Helping, but Stressful, Profession

After reading this chapter, you should understand the following:

- How your profession affects your stress level

- How your philosophy of corrections is important to managing stress

- Why corrections, due to unique stress and stressors, may be a helping job, but not the "dream job"

- How the offender subculture affects you and causes stress

Correctional workers need to understand how their profession contributes to stress. Corrections is a human-services profession. Like nursing, education, medicine, and day care, corrections provides services to the community. However, corrections ranks high among jobs as being very stressful, and those who work with offenders see that daily. In Great Britain in 1985, the University of Manchester conducted a study of 150 jobs, ranking them from the most stressful to the least stressful. The results were based on participants' self-reporting. The most stressful jobs according to stress levels were as follows (Moynahan, 1999):

- miners
- police
- pilots, prison officers, construction workers, journalists
- dentists, advertising employees
- actors
- politicians

- physicians, tax collectors

Correctional officers, probation and parole officers, and support staff provide the following specific services to offenders: housing; sanitation; food; protection from other offenders; access to the legal system; access to commissary and recreational activities; treatment for mental health or substance-abuse problems; educational and vocational training; religious programs; counseling and guidance; medical and dental treatment; access to community agencies prior to release, and visiting. Corrections professionals perform a valuable public service by keeping the public safe by incarcerating offenders and steering them away from crime upon release. Corrections professionals hold the public's trust and it is a burden that they cannot forget.

Whether incarcerated or under supervision, an offender's world is controlled primarily by corrections professionals. Jail and prison officers control the movement and daily routine of inmates in their care. Probation and parole officers must be notified when clients want to move or change jobs. Support correctional staff, such as medical, food service, maintenance, and clerical workers, affects inmates' diet, environment, and health care. All correctional workers serve the community by keeping offenders under proper supervision and preventing escapes and further crime.

Understanding Correctional Philosophies

Correctional workers will find it helpful to understand how different philosophical approaches to corrections can affect their job and the stress they may feel. Each correctional officer, counselor, or probation officer has a philosophy about corrections. The following are some popular approaches (Allen and Simonsen, 2004):

1. Punishment. Offenders are enemies of society and should be punished severely for willful law breaking. Some officers lump all inmates into the category of "society's rejects." According to this approach, most inmates deserve lengthy sentences and are incapable of being rehabilitated.

2. Treatment. Offenders have problems, which should be recognized and treated. Some feel that although incarceration is necessary in some cases, most offenders have problems, such as substance abuse, mental disorders, or lack of job skills that can be remedied by participation in rehabilitative treatment programs. Correctional workers embracing this treatment ideology believe in helping the offender and enter their jobs with a commitment to these principles.

3. Prevention. Some, although not all, crime could be prevented if programs focused on individuals and the environment in which they live. Corrections professionals in treatment programs try to help offenders overcome their problems so that they will find alternatives to a life of crime. Prevention programs, such as jail tours for high school students and diversion programs that give offenders a second chance, appeal to corrections professionals who support this ideology.

It is important to know with which ideology you are comfortable. For example, if you are a correctional officer who embraces the philosophy of punishment, then being placed in a treatment position may cause you much stress. If, on the other hand, you are a counselor who has a strong commitment to treatment and rehabilitation, being transferred to a custody position would be upsetting. Often, correctional workers, especially officers in jails and prisons, are transferred and moved around. Supervisors should be aware that these transfers can cause stress because of conflicting ideologies. If agency policy and procedure dictate these transfers take place, management and workers must work together to persuade the affected worker that a variety of approaches can be beneficial—to the worker, to the offender, and to the community.

Concerning stress management, you may be in a treatment position where the agency heads believe more in custody and control. Your views are not necessarily ruled out, but you may feel out of place, or reduced in importance. Some staff become negative and seethe and steam about it. The best way to deal with it is to talk to your supervisor to clarify your role and how you should function.

A Basic Understanding of Corrections

There are a few fundamental aspects about corrections that workers should understand:

1. There will always be more offenders than staff to supervise them.

2. People do not like being held against their will, being closely supervised, or told what to do.

3. Corrections staff is the point of contact for many people—including supervisors, offenders, attorneys, and offenders' families—each with their specific needs or demands.

4. To work in corrections, one must be multitask oriented, or more simply, able to handle many assignments or tasks simultaneously.

5. There is a physical risk when in close proximity to offenders, ranging from death, to assault, to contracting a communicable disease, such as HIV, hepatitis B and C, tuberculosis, and so forth.

More Offenders than Staff

There never seems to be enough help. Each area of corrections is affected by the large numbers of offenders involved in the criminal justice system. Jails, for example, are designed to provide secure confinement to inmates while operating with minimum staff. For example, one or two jail officers may work a floor containing fifteen cell-blocks holding five inmates each. As a result, two officers are watching seventy-five inmates. To the jail staff, it may seem as if the squad or team is always short staffed. The high inmate-to-staff ratio increases the concern many officers have about the danger of the job. After all, dangerous situations, assaults, or arguments can happen with little or no notice.

In the probation and parole area, the numbers are not much better. Caseload figures from different studies indicate that the ratio of parolees per parole officer may be as high as 117 to one (American Correctional Association, 2004). Probation officers also suffer from the stress of large caseloads. In 2003, an average caseload of 112 probationers—each with his or her own set of problems, behaviors, and concerns— was assigned to probation officers (American Correctional Association, 2004).

More current research suggests that there is no optimum figure for a probation officer's caseload. This is possibly due to different models of caseload management, such as assigning intensive supervision cases to one specific group in the agency (Champion, 2002). Probation and parole officers often quickly burn out due to large caseloads and low pay. What is frustrating to most probation or parole officers is the knowledge that many offenders do not get the attention and supervision they need.

Probation and parole officers are also hit with a "double blast": not only do they have to supervise a large caseload, but they also have to submit presentence investigation reports (PSIs). PSIs include information such as offenders' criminal histories, background, and the current offense. PSIs are written under deadlines and require a lot of work on tight schedules. (In fact, PSI deadlines often dictate when a probation or parole officer can take vacations, further complicating stress management.) Defense attorneys receive copies, which they can object to, causing the probation or parole officer to take more time to answer the attorneys' objections. Many probation officers say they cannot take vacations or ever completely relax, knowing that their workloads are increasing while they are away.

Correctional support staff, such as medical staff, clerks, secretaries, food service workers, and maintenance technicians, also face a lot of strain as institutional populations increase. Their staff numbers never keep pace with the number of inmates. For example, in a county jail rated for a capacity of 600, the clerical staff consists of five clerks. If the population doubles, the same five clerks will handle double the work-load. The same is true for food service workers, medical staff, and maintenance personnel. One often-overlooked aspect of crowded facilities is the enormous strain on electrical and plumbing systems. In crowded facilities, blown circuits and plumbing-fixture breakdowns occur more frequently, adding to the stress of both staff and inmates.

No One Likes To Be Held Against His or Her Will

Correctional workers always must remember that no matter what inmates or clients say or how cooperative they may appear, they dislike being incarcerated or supervised. Why is this so important to remember? Offenders generally will try to make their situation more comfortable by manipulating other inmates and staff. One of the biggest stressors in correctional work is falling victim to offenders' "con games" or keeping your guard up against offenders' stories of family problems, childhood woes, and his or her own victimization by society. Other than an escape or suicide, nothing makes correctional workers doubt their self-confidence more than being manipulated by offenders (*see* Cornelius' *Art of the Con* [2001]).

Correctional Staff Are a Primary Point of Contact

Correctional workers, especially counselors, officers, and probation and parole officers, perform many different tasks that require them to interact with many different people. In an institution, officers working in cellblocks must answer to the needs and concerns of the inmates in their areas, in addition to responding to requests from institutional counselors, support staff, supervisors, volunteers, visitors, and inmates' attorneys. During one shift, for example, an officer may handle instructions from the classification staff to move several inmates and help search the cellblock. After the morning count, an attorney arrives to consult with an inmate, requiring the officer to escort the inmate to the visiting area. In the midst of all these demands, the officer has to be constantly on guard against escape or inmate assaults. Classification counselors also have excessive demands on them: conducting intake interviews, handling inmates with special needs, preparing for and attending disciplinary hearings, and so forth.

They must consult with the mental health and medical staffs when making assignments and trouble-shooting complaints or requests from inmates, probation officers, attorneys, and inmates' families. In fact, every job in an institution requires interaction with other members of the criminal justice system.

Probation officers also must interact with many people. Probation officers perform tasks, such as writing presentence investigation reports, conducting home or job visits, finding employment for offenders, and performing crisis intervention in domestic disputes.

Parole officers must keep detailed records of offenders' progress and contacts and interact with offenders' employers, treatment therapists, and parole boards (Champion, 1990).

Multiple Roles of Correctional Officers

Patrol officer

Security specialist

Legal adviser

Parent or authority figure

Investigator of complaints of theft, assault, harassment, sexual activities, and criminal acts

Surveillance officer, patrolling inmate housing areas, enforcing regulations

Inmate advisor—answering inmates' questions about their sentences, court appearances, and personal issues

Inmate representative at adjustment hearings

Inmate coach—helping immature inmates

Teacher of better hygiene

Role model

Judge

Information agent—answering inmates' questions concerning programs, facility rules, education, jobs needs, housing, lack of child care, and so forth

Diplomat

Counselor

Participant in disciplinary hearings

Intervening force in inmate disputes

Crisis-intervention expert

Court advisor/investigator

Social worker

Problem-solving adviser

Referral agent helping inmates get linked with community programs or resources

Correctional workers' jobs are not narrowly defined. Correctional workers have many different roles—most of which are not listed in their job descriptions. Having to jump from role to role can increase the stress corrections professionals feel. It is important to understand these diverse roles (*see* the prior chart). With multiple roles come multiple demands due to interactions with many people and situations. Workers have to quickly adapt from one role to the other. During a single day, a probation officer may intercede in a family fight during a home visit, receive an urgent telephone call from a judge requesting a conference about a PSI, and end the day with a client's employer who is angry about the offender being placed in jail because of a probation revocation.

Stress is a part of corrections work no matter what the situation.

The "Dream Job"

Many corrections professionals initially have high ideals about helping offenders. Corrections is a "people"-type job, where staff seldom sit all day at a desk. We deal with offenders all day, every day. Many of us entered this work because we like working with people. This frame of mind is called the "Dream Job" (Veninga and Spradley, 1981). Although belief in the dream job may spur correctional staff or probation officers to work long hours and aggressively face whatever problems come their way, workers with this mindset rarely are prepared for the lack of appreciation of their efforts. Many correctional employees start out believing that offenders will appreciate what is being done for them. Unfortunately, nothing could be further from the truth! Soon, however, workers realize that offenders' con games, ingratitude, and manipulation are more often the rule than are expressions of gratitude. This reality shoots big holes in the dream job and may add to a worker's stress. However, on a stressful day, we do not want to see offenders or deal with them, but we must. It is part of the job.

Understanding the Offender Subculture

Correctional workers, at least once in their careers, usually ask themselves why offenders can't be like law-abiding people. Instead of becoming frustrated by trying to answer an impossible question, workers should try to understand the offender subculture. Aspects of this subculture are offenders' personality traits, immaturely coping with life's problems, and moral differences between offenders and workers. Workers should have a basic understanding of these three areas.

Personality Traits

Offenders exhibit the following personality characteristics (Perdue, 1983):

- feelings of inferiority, inadequacy, low self-esteem
- the need for attention (more than other adults)
- impatience
- the tendency to rationalize their behavior
- high rates of substance abuse
- lack of responsibility and values

It is no secret that most offenders make up excuses for their behavior, exhibit impatience when making requests, and behave irresponsibly. The key is for workers not to let these traits surprise them and subsequently become a stressor.

The nerve-wracking aspect of taking a human-service attitude to correctional work is that correctional workers must take the cards that are dealt—clientele are assigned to probation and parole officers, correctional officers must handle whatever offenders are assigned to their housing units, and intake officers cannot pick and choose which offenders are to be interviewed. Correctional workers must take what is given. As one jail officer said:

> *When I worked booking and then moved into classification, one thing that stressed me out is that I never knew what type of offender I would meet and have to deal with. You kind of get used to it, but at times you do feel powerless. I could come from interviewing a calm, cooperative inmate to having to deal with an offender vomiting or throwing feces. One shift I phoned my wife and held up the phone so she could hear all of the screaming and door banging, plus an inmate singing Frank Sinatra tunes. I told her: "Now, you understand why I am the way I am when I get home."*

Stressors in Corrections Work

A common denominator to many stressors affecting corrections professionals is a lack of control. The worker has to learn to cope with this. The following items are just some of the stressors with which most institutional corrections professionals must handle:

- substandard salaries
- tight deadlines

- shift work

- short staffing

- inmate demands

- inmate arguments

- argumentative inmate families and attorneys

- court appearances

- internal affairs investigations

- substandard buildings and equipment

- lack of clear guidelines or written procedures

- conflicting decisions from supervisors

- conflicting operations among shifts

- lack of support from supervisors

- no recognition for good work

- lack of input in decision making

- inadequate training

- poor communication

- feelings of failure due to inmates not seeming to benefit from your efforts

- lack of promotional opportunities

- boredom

- high staff turnover

- large caseloads

- bureaucratic "red tape" and paperwork

- cramped working conditions

- excessive noise and unpleasant odors

- exposure to body fluids or feces

- offender "con games," lies, and manipulation

- emergencies (fires, power outages)

- on-the-job injuries from inmate assaults, possibility of on-duty death

- presentence report guidelines

- aggressive, violent inmates or clients

- inmates who are suffering from mental disorders

- inmates under the influence of alcohol/drugs

- being sued or being a target of an inmate grievance
- escapes

The stressors that affect probation or parole officers are comparable. Here is a "thumbnail sketch" of sources of stress for probation or parole officers (Champion, 2002):

- job dissatisfaction: low pay, large caseloads, unchallenging work988
- role conflict: rehabilitation and enforcement
- role ambiguity: lack of a mission or agency goals
- officer/client interactions: work overload, client and probation/parole officer may be mismatched
- excessive paperwork and performance measures: large caseloads and increased responsibility means more documentation, more research, more follow up, and more paperwork with strict due dates
- low self-esteem and public image: seen as inept, especially when a client re-offends and probation or parole officer is overworked
- job risks and liabilities: home visits on the offenders' "turf," risk of assault
- liabilities include giving poor advice, violating the offender's privacy.

To clearly illustrate how the corrections field is stressful, this author, with the assistance of the American Correctional Association and George Mason University, compiled statistical data from a questionnaire (*see* Appendix F) sent to randomly selected correctional agencies in mid 2002. In examining the responses from probation/parole officers, jail officers, and prison officers, the top ten stress symptoms by job category are shown in Figure 3.1 on the next page.

Although Chapter 1 discussed the symptoms of stress, the survey respondents reported these most frequent symptoms:

- headaches
- impatience
- anxiety
- sleep difficulties
- fatigue/low energy
- cannot relax
- anger
- poor concentration
- back and neck pain

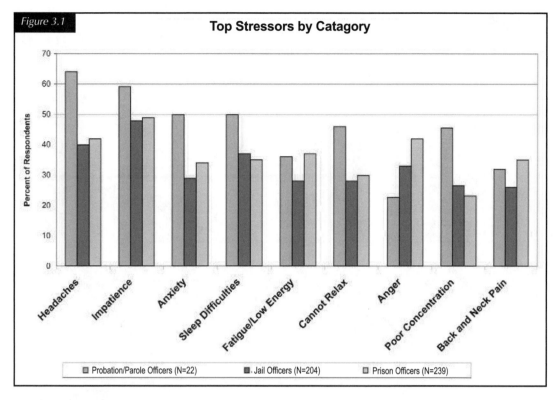

Figure 3.1

Top Stressors by Catagory

More than 60 percent of probation and parole officers and more than 40 percent of jail and prison officers reported headaches. High numbers of responders indicated impatience and sleep difficulties. All of the reported symptoms, if not dealt with, make working in corrections difficult.

The stressors causing these symptoms are shown in Figure 3.2 on page 40:

- short staffing
- lazy colleagues
- conflicting decisions from supervisors
- poor communication
- no recognition for good work
- lack of support from supervisors
- conflicting operations among shifts
- large caseload
- tight deadlines
- lack of input in decision making
- low salary
- bureaucratic red tape/paperwork

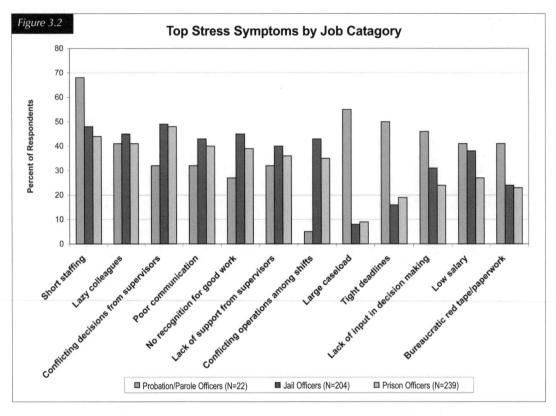

Figure 3.2

Top Stress Symptoms by Job Catagory

□ Probation/Parole Officers (N=22)　■ Jail Officers (N=204)　□ Prison Officers (N=239)

Probation/parole officers listed short staffing, large caseloads, and tight deadlines in more than 50 percent of their responses. Almost 50 percent of jail and prison officers listed conflicting decisions from supervisors as a major stressor.

How is this stress problem illustrated in a way for all to see? Consider these findings by the National Institute of Justice (Finn, 2000):

- Many correctional officers refuse to answer their home telephones because it may be the facility calling them into work for overtime. Some officers get a second, unlisted line or cell phone that they keep secret from their agency.

- From 1990 to 1995, the number of attacks on correctional officers in state and federal prisons increased by almost one-third during a time when the number of correctional officers increased by only 14 percent.

- A common view by correctional officers is that the public is clueless as to what correctional officers do, and ask such things as "if they beat inmates all the time." Many do not say when asked what their job is, just saying that they work for the county, work for the state, and so forth. Subsequently, they feel isolated from family and friends at social gatherings.

- With the exception of police officers, the number of nonfatal workplace incidents is higher per 1,000 employees for correctional officers than any other profession, including taxi drivers, convenience store workers, mental health workers, and teachers.

- Family relationships are damaged, sometimes beyond repair. Workers displace their anger and frustrations on to their families, telling children to go to their "cells" or locking a child out of his room and searching it.

The end result is that we have a group of dedicated professionals in all areas of corrections working and trying to both perform a public service and help people in a job setting full of stressors. Some workers feel like they are in a vice or trying to climb a hill that is impossible to climb.

Not all stress comes from the offenders, supervisors, or the physical plant of the facility. Many people who enter corrections have a sense of pride and public service. Correctional officers take pride in the uniform and what it represents, and probation and parole officers try to help offenders. However, two stressors from outside the system recently have been reported (Finn, 2000):

- **Poor public image:** Correctional officers are seen as brutal, animalistic "hicks" who senselessly abuse inmates, and probation/parole officers are seen as inept, overworked bureaucrats who cannot keep an eye on offenders.

- **Poor pay:** Many officers report low pay as a stressor. In one state, the starting salary for correctional officers is $12,000. In another state, officers start at $18,000 and the most that they can earn after eighteen months is $26,400. In one privately owned correctional facility, the starting pay was $14,000 to $16,000 per year (Finn, 2000; American Correctional Association, 2003). A quick look at correctional officer's salaries in 2002 reveals that the average salary at the end of their probationary period was $26,807. (Camp, 2002). In some areas where the cost of living is high, correctional staff struggle to make ends meet, work overtime, or work extra jobs—all of which can add to stress.

  Probation and parole officers are also concerned about pay. The overall average pay in 2002 for a probation and parole officer was $38,501. The 2002 average entry-level pay was approximately $29,214 per year. Also, most jurisdictions require a bachelor's degree for an entry-level position, which means that many new probation or parole officers have the burden of paying off student loans (Champion, 2002; Camp and Camp, 1999). To advance their careers, many probation and parole officers go back to college to obtain a master's degree or obtain licensing in counseling and substance-abuse counseling.

Pay and public image are important. The job is stressful enough, and it hurts and demoralizes corrections professionals when they are seen as substandard, unethical people who cannot do what the public perceives is a simple job—like "just sitting around and watching inmates all day." Coupled with that is low or below-average pay. Pay rates are based on the revenue of the jurisdiction and funding from the state. It is hard to raise a family or continue an education on the public servant's pay of a correctional professional.

One stress-management instructor, also a veteran jail officer, says:

> *In every stress management class that I teach for both officers and probation and parole officers, I ask them what stresses them out. One answer that always comes back for discussion is the lack of money, or the bills piling up. These folks are not extravagant and do not appear to waste their money. It is obvious that they take pride in their work but have trouble making ends meet. They have families. You can tell that they are strained.*

Coping Maturely with Life's Problems

Everyone encounters problems through life—disagreements, job losses, debts, births, deaths, divorce, criticisms, and other stressors. How people cope or deal with these problems tells others how mature they are. Mature, adult people do not exhibit behavior that gets them arrested. According to sociologist Robert Johnson (1987), mature coping consists of three characteristics: solving problems through legitimate means, dealing with problems without lying or violence, and assisting others in need.

Solving problems through legitimate means

For example, if John's rent doubles, he—as a law-abiding citizen—will cope by asking his boss for a raise or by cutting back on other expenses. He is using legitimate means to solve his problem. Don, a criminal with a long arrest record, may deal differently with the problem. He may start embezzling money from his job or dealing drugs. In other words, he uses illegitimate means to solve the problem.

Offenders often deny that a problem, such as alcoholism or drug dependency, exists. Subsequently, they resist counseling. Their resistance and denial only makes correctional workers' jobs tougher. Offenders will argue with staff about being placed in rehabilitation programs, claiming they do not need them.

Dealing with problems without lying or violence

Mature people do not lie or use violence to solve problems. Many offenders both lie and use violence to settle conflicts. Inmates in prisons get into fights over gambling debts, stolen property, or which television show they get to watch. Offenders on probation or parole may take out frustrations by physically abusing their spouse or children. These incidents often result in probation or parole revocations.

Assisting others in need

One other trait of a mature person is to assist others in need and to understand their feelings. Mature adults help others and, in doing so, make their lives more gratifying. However, this help does not have any strings or conditions attached. For example, law-abiding citizens will do something for a neighbor, such as help fix an appliance, offer a ride to work, or feed a pet while the neighbor is away, without holding the neighbor accountable to return the favor. Favors are done because a need for help was there. Offenders generally will hold other offenders accountable for "favors," such as expecting a return of borrowed cigarettes.

Moral Differences Between Offenders and Workers

People enter the field of corrections for various reasons. For some, it is a secure job (there will always be criminals who will need to be locked up) or a stepping stone to another position in the criminal justice system, such as being a police officer or eventually becoming a warden. For others, it presents a chance to help people.

The opportunity to help people is why many correctional workers stay in the field despite the stress and strain. However, the desire to help can be self-defeating. Some workers become overly involved with offenders in their charge. These workers want to help too much and as a result, they work long hours and perform many tasks offenders could do themselves. Correctional workers who fall into this dilemma are trying hard to impress their own moral code on a population that already has chosen different ethical standards. Correctional workers must realize that offenders may not always measure up to their high standards. At best, all that can be hoped for is an apparent positive change in the offender—a change that reflects a desire to act appropriately and live a crime-free life.

Another aspect of corrections work that has become noteworthy is offender manipulation. Corrections work, either inside a facility or in the community, requires workers to be at the top of their game. However, there are days when we may not feel quite up to par. However, the toll that unmanaged stress takes can create targets for the manipulator. Consider these examples:

- An officer is going through a divorce and is under a lot of stress. She is overheard by inmates talking to a colleague about it. The next thing she knows, inmates want to be her new support group and will feign a lot of sympathy to get friendly with her. They hope to control her and get her to do favors for her new "friends."

- A prison cook is having financial difficulties. Inmates find out about this, because under stress and wanting to talk to someone, the cook reveals his problem. They start persuading him to bring in drugs and promise that he will be paid some "good money."

- A probation officer's spouse passes away, and in her grief, she gets behind on her caseload. A streetwise client makes a romantic play for her so she will over-look infractions.

- Due to the boredom associated with burnout, a veteran officer becomes sloppy on searches, headcounts, and paperwork.

Whenever an employee is disgruntled, is having problems at home, or is burned out, the offenders will pick up on this and move in with schemes and ploys to try to get their way. The offender should not know an individual's personal business and when he or she is under stress. They will become this individual's new support group. Stress management does guard against the manipulator. Practice good stress management and get training in resisting manipulation (Cornelius, 2001).

Coping with Stress

After reading this chapter, you should understand the following:

- How harmful physical and mental coping strategies affect you

- How to develop positive physical and mental coping strategies

- How anger can affect you and those around you

- How to effectively manage your anger

- How to put balance into your life

To effectively manage stress, correctional workers need to learn how to cope with the stress in their daily lives. Some coping strategies work, some do not. Stress management is effective only when workers are knowledgeable about the benefits of the methods they choose.

To cope with stress, workers should be able to identify stressors in their lives, understand the feelings the stressors generate, and know the effectiveness of the coping strategies they have chosen. Although some coping methods may be appealing and easy (such as eating fast food frequently or skipping going to the gym), it is important to understand that some methods actually can be more harmful than beneficial.

Defining Coping

In the dictionary, "cope" means "to struggle [with] and not fail." Another way to look at coping is to say when one copes with something, one deals with it. The bottom line is that to cope means to do something about a problem. Unmanaged stress, especially for correctional staff, is a problem. The problem is knowing whether your choice of action is the most beneficial. Managing stress means coping with stress by choosing positive methods to improve body and mind. Not only can coping be positive (beneficial) or negative (harmful), coping can mean developing physical and mental strategies for dealing with stress. How a corrections professional copes with stress will determine:

- his or her quality of physical health
- his or her quality of mental or behavioral health
- the overall quality of his or her life

Coping in the physical sense means doing something to relieve or minimize the effects of stress on your body. In the mental area, it means doing something to relieve stress on your mind.

Attitudes Toward Stress

The following five observations represent a cross-section of ways different corrections professionals deal with stress. Some workers have a positive outlook; others do not. Having a positive attitude has a large effect on your ability to manage stress.

"You have to constantly generate positive feelings where the negative is all around you."

Deputy Sheriff (Maltagliati, 1987)

"You just accept it. Some days it's eating. Some days it's drinking. You can't really deal with it, that's the most disheartening thing.

Prison Officer (Lombardo, 1987)

"I come in jammed [under influence of drugs] every day. That's the way I handle this place [prison]."

Prison Officer (Kauffman, 1988)

"When you first start the job [in a correctional facility], you take (inmate comments and stares) personally. But there is a certain callousness that takes place. After a while it just goes right through you…. Because if you take it [stress] home with you—forget it. It [stress] will ruin your life, your friends' lives. Some people learn it the hard way. Some people never learn it."

Jail Officer: male (Manry, 2003)

"I think that it's [the job] more of a mental stress than a physical stress or any-thing. . . . It's always having your guard up, always being on your toes. At the end of the day you're mentally exhausted, not really physically exhausted. That's one of the things that's hard. That's part of it."

Jail officer: female (Manry, 2003)

Physical Coping

To deal with stress effectively, adaptive energy must be recharged and maintained through good health habits, such as eating a proper diet and getting enough rest and regular exercise. Unfortunately, many workers engage in negative-coping mechanisms that hurt them physically, such as overeating, choosing poor nutrition, smoking, abus-ing substances, and not exercising.

Overeating

Workers often believe that the way to feel relief from stress is to eat big meals and junk food. Not only is overeating dangerous, but so is the weight gained as a result. More weight means more strain on your cardiovascular system during the stress reac-tion. One correctional officer gained fifty pounds from overeating during his rookie year (Cheek, 1984). In 1985, 20 to 40 percent of the adult U.S. population had a weight problem (Wood, 1985). Recently, the U.S. Surgeon General reported that:

- Nearly two-out-of-three adults in the United States are overweight or obese, and the number is increasing.

- An estimated 1,200 people die daily from weight-related illnesses, totaling approximately 300,000 deaths per year, more than deaths annually from pneu-monia, motor vehicle accidents, and airline crashes combined.

- Health-care costs for overweight conditions and obesity total $117 billion annually. (Squires, 2001).

In a 2004 TIME/ABC News Poll, 58 percent of Americans polled said that they would like to lose weight, but only 36 percent are following a diet plan. Surprisingly, only 26 percent exercise at least three times per week. When asked to choose a particular cause of obesity in the United States, the number one cause according to the poll was not getting enough physical exercise, at 86 percent, closely followed by poor eating habits at 84 percent (Lemonick, 2004).

Proper diet and exercise are essential to proper weight control and if one or both of these areas are out of balance, the worker will experience problems with weight. In a high-pressure field such as corrections, workers must look and feel their best to command respect, have a positive self-image, and stay healthy. Eating sensibly is important. Workers must resist the temptation to "pig out" on high-fat foods after a stressful day. Eating a big meal, sacking out on the couch, and not exercising is not the way to keep a body healthy for stress management.

Poor Nutrition

Many workers believe that a doughnut and coffee in the morning for breakfast is good enough. They also may believe that a big burger, fries, and a cola make a good lunch, which they follow with a big dinner and a rich dessert. What they are doing is substituting commonsense eating habits for food and drink that taste good and are fun to eat. For some workers, it is easier and quicker to order a pizza for dinner than to cook a dinner with healthy, nutritious foods. In today's society, it is easy, fast, and convenient to eat foods that are not good for us.

Your diet should be well balanced, but low in fat. You should eat fruits, vegetables, whole grains, lean meat, fish and other seafood, and poultry. Limit the fast foods you consume. If you drink a lot of milk (which is good for you), drink low fat or skim milk instead of whole milk.

Follow your common sense with eating, as with all activities. You do not have to give up fun-to-eat food entirely, just eat it moderately. Pay close attention to the following foods, which, when consumed excessively, can be harmful:

- coffee/caffeinated drinks (such as colas)
- chocolate
- high-sugar foods
- high-fat foods

Coffee

Although the caffeine in coffee can give a "lift" and improve alertness, coffee may not be beneficial. Research indicates that more than three cups per day can cause digestive upset. Drinking coffee late at night can disrupt sleep. Other reported effects from drinking a lot of coffee include an irregular heartbeat, headaches, irritability, muscle tension, insomnia, and possibly increased risk of heart attack. As workers drink more coffee, they develop a tolerance that reduces the stimulating effects they like. Remember, too, that many soft drink colas contain caffeine.

Chocolate

Often workers head for the vending machine to get a chocolate bar, which gives them an energy boost due to its sugar content. But an insulin "backlash" can cause irritability, fatigue, and sluggishness. Chocolate also contains caffeine.

High-sugar foods

Powdered doughnuts, cream-filled cakes, and chocolate cupcakes are high in calories and fat. These foods are available everywhere, from stop-and-go convenience stores to vending machines. Although these foods will stop hunger and give a temporary energy boost, they may make you lethargic in the long run.

High-fat foods

Eating foods high in fat and cholesterol can seriously weaken your heart. If high-fat foods are constantly consumed, the bloodstream's fat content will increase. Increased blood fats can result in arteriosclerosis (a narrowing of the blood vessels due to plaque—an accumulation of blood fats and cholesterol on the vessel wall). This, in turn, can lead to coronary heart disease, which is the leading cause of premature deaths among Americans (Powell, 1992). One tool in stress management is to be aware of the level of your cholesterol, which you should have checked by a doctor. Lipoproteins are the substances that transport cholesterol around the body. The type of lipoproteins and the risk of heart disease from cholesterol are related in three types of cholesterol (Cooper and Cooper, 1996):

1. <u>HDL:</u> This is high density lipoprotein or good cholesterol. HDL protects the heart and cardiac system by drawing cholesterol away from the coronary arteries. The higher your blood HDL level, the better protected you are from heart disease.

2. <u>LDL:</u> Called the bad cholesterol, or plaque, LDL (low density lipoprotein) combines with other blood-borne chemicals and sticks to the walls of coronary arteries, especially near the heart. This leads to the formation of a substance that clogs arteries, plaque. The higher the blood HDL level, the higher the risk for heart disease.

3. <u>VLDL:</u> Manufactured by the liver, VLDL, or very low density lipoprotein, transports various fatty acids including triglycerides and VLDL throughout the body. Triglycerides are free fatty acids that are stored in the body as fat. The higher the VLDL level, the more LDL is produced by the liver. VLDL is linked to the manufacture of LDL, fat transport, and fat storage. The bottom line is that the higher the VLDL, the more bad cholesterol (LDL) that is produced.

According to the American Heart Association, everyone who is age twenty and older should have their cholesterol levels checked every five years. The American Heart Association recommends a "lipoprotein profile" test performed after a nine-to-twelve-hour fast to obtain information about your total cholesterol, your LDL cholesterol, your HDL cholesterol, and your triglycerides, which is another type of fat in your blood. If your total cholesterol is at 200 mg/dl (milligrams per deciliter of blood) or more, and your HDL is less than 40 mg/dl, a lipoprotein profile test is necessary (American Heart Association, 2004). If you are serious about cholesterol, please look at the following information.

Total cholesterol: A desirable level is less than 200 mg/dl, but a borderline high level is considered to be 200-239 mg/dl. A high level is at 240 mg/dl and above.

LDL (Bad cholesterol): Less than 100 mg/dl is considered optimal, and 100-129 mg/dl is near /above optimal. Borderline high levels are 130-159 mg/dl, high levels are 160-189 mg/dl, and very high is 190 mg/dl and above.

Triglycerides: Treatment may be necessary for levels of 150-199 mg/dl (borderline high) and 200 mg/dl or more (high). (American Heart Association, 2004)

Age and gender can affect cholesterol levels. As men and women age, their cholesterol levels increase. After menopause, women's LDL levels tend to increase. You cannot do anything about age, gender, or family history, as our genes determine how much cholesterol our bodies make. High-cholesterol levels can run in families. But you can do something about cholesterol by eating a diet low in saturated fats and cholesterol, losing weight (which lowers total cholesterol), and being physically active. Keeping your weight down and engaging in regular physical activity lowers LDL cholesterol and triglycerides and raises HDL cholesterol. The American Heart Association recommends that a person should be engaging in physical activity for thirty minutes a day on most if not all days (American Heart Association, 2004).

Diabetes Alert

High-sugar foods, such as candy bars and sugared doughnuts, often provide instant gratification and a temporary energy boost. But beware. The "boost" is from sugars being released into the blood. This triggers the pancreas to release insulin, which lowers the blood-sugar level as sugar is removed and sent to the liver. The liver stores sugars in a form your body can use. The more refined the sugar (pastries, candy bars), the more insulin is released. If too much insulin is released, you can feel tired, dizzy, and irritable. This reaction often stimulates an increased desire for more sugar. Diabetes can result from the continued strain on the pancreas (Whittlesey, 1986;

McQuade and Aikman, 1974). According to the Diabetes Prevention Program, Type 2 diabetes (which is linked to obesity) can be prevented by maintaining a diet that limits fats to 25 percent and engaging in regular exercise (Squires, 2002).

Smoking

Many workers "relax" with a cigarette, pipe, cigar, or chewing tobacco. Sometimes tobacco is combined with a cup of coffee, unleashing a double blast of two stimulants—nicotine and caffeine. Keep in mind that instead of helping yourself, you really are ingesting poisons into your body: tar and nicotine.

According to researchers, the nicotine found in tobacco products stimulates the body to produce hormones, such as adrenaline. Alertness is increased and the person feels less anxious and more energetic. People often smoke cigarettes to cope with daily stress and feel that they cannot perform their jobs without smoking cigarettes. In correctional systems that have not gone smoke-free, some officers "light up" constantly during their shift and some probation officers cannot type a pre-sentence investigation report without having a pack of cigarettes nearby. After a critical incident in a prison, such as an assault, officers often go for a cup of coffee and a smoke, thus putting two stimulants into their bodies when instead they should be letting their bodies calm down.

Smoking can ruin your health. An estimated 430,700 Americans die each year from smoking-related diseases. Annually in the United States, smoking costs 97.2 billion dollars in health care costs and lost productivity. Smoking is directly responsible for 87 percent of lung cancer cases in the United States. Smoking also causes most cases of lung diseases such as chronic bronchitis and emphysema (American Lung Association, 2004).

Smoking impairs blood circulation and breathing. Workers subject to high stress need their blood to circulate and their breathing to be strong and unimpaired. What good is a correctional officer who, after hearing of a disturbance in a cellblock, runs up two flights of stairs to help, but is out of breath when he or she gets there? Smoking is deadly, not only to the worker, but also to coworkers who need assistance and backup. One key question about smoking: after a stressful incident, such as an inmate assault, arresting a parole violator, and so forth, you should be returning to the pre-stress calm state, so why ingest a powerful stimulant such as nicotine?

Good Reasons to Quit

If you are thinking about quitting, but still are undecided, then consider the following facts about smoking (Rich, 1993):

- One out of every five deaths in the United States can be attributed to smoking
- Cardiovascular disease is the number one cause of death caused by smoking, followed by lung cancer, and respiratory disease
- Smokers' life expectancies are on average five years less than those who do not smoke

After You Quit Smoking

It is amazing what happens to you after you put out your last cigarette. Within twenty minutes, your blood pressure and pulse will return to normal. Carbon-monoxide levels within your blood also will return to normal within this time. After eight hours, the oxygen level in your blood will return to normal. After twenty-four hours, your chances of suffering a heart attack decrease, and nicotine leaves your body within forty-eight to seventy-two hours after your last cigarette. During the next two days through nine months, your circulation, lung capacity, and energy levels increase. At the same time, coughing, sinus congestion, and shortness of breath decrease. Within ten years, precancerous cells are replaced (Hunt, 1994).

Substance Abuse

Criminals are not the only ones in society who abuse alcohol and drugs. Correctional workers also are prone to substance abuse—drinking to excess or using drugs as a way to cope with stress.

Alcohol is the most widely used—and abused—drug in our society (McQuade and Aikman, 1974). Alcoholic beverages are cheap, easily available, and socially acceptable. In updated research from the National Institute on Alcohol Abuse and Alcoholism, American adults who abuse alcohol or are alcohol dependent increased from 7.4 percent in 1991-1992 to nearly 8.5 percent in 2001-2002 (National Institute on Alcohol Abuse and Alcoholism, 2004).

Alcohol abuse and dependency are not good combatants in battling stress. According to the National Institute on Alcohol Abuse and Alcoholism, alcohol abuse is a condition characterized by:

- failure to fulfill major role obligations and tasks at work, school, and at home
- interpersonal social and legal problems

- drinking in hazardous situations

Alcohol dependence or alcoholism is characterized by:

- impaired/lack of control over one's drinking
- preoccupation with drinking
- developing a tolerance to alcohol and/or withdrawal symptoms

  (National Institute on Alcohol Abuse and Alcoholism, 2004)

All of these characteristics can have a negative effect on correctional worker's employment, social, and home life. When life is stressful enough, alcohol is not the way to cope.

When used moderately, alcohol can help workers unwind and relax (Whittlesey, 1986). One or two drinks per day, usually up to two ounces of alcohol total, are all right for some workers. Problems arise when drinking more than this amount becomes a daily stress-coping mechanism in lieu of other positive-coping strategies. For example, a probation officer going home after a stressful day has four or five beers to relax, instead of having just one (or even none) and taking a long, leisurely walk. A jail officer believes that to relax, she has to go out every night after work with coworkers and spend a few hours drinking while her husband and children wait for her at home.

When alcohol is abused, health problems, such as heart disease, raised blood pressure, brain dysfunction, cancer, and sleep problems may arise (Benson et al., 1987). Many problem drinkers become alcoholics, which in turn can lead to malnutrition, blackouts, disrupted home life, and job inefficiency. And if you are trying to keep your weight down, keep in mind that alcohol is high in calories, but low in nutrition. Correctional workers, especially, should know from dealing with offenders the effects of alcohol abuse. Yet, many continue to cope by drinking heavily, saying that "it can't happen to me" or "it won't happen to me." But—it does!

Like alcohol, prescription drugs can be abused and used as a negative-coping mechanism. Many Americans use tranquilizers to relax, calm down, and relieve the pressure and stress of everyday living. Valium, and similar drugs designed to reduce stress, can effectively reduce anxiety and stress in the short term. If used chronically for long periods of time, however, addiction may develop. When a "hooked" worker tries to stop, he or she may experience anxiety, nervousness, taste and smell distortions, and difficulty sleeping. If Valium or other tranquilizers need to be taken, they should be taken for less than three to four weeks in small doses. If Valium must be taken continuously, the worker should take frequent breaks from it (Powell, 1992). Using tranquilizers, such as Valium, should only be a last resort, and should be used only under a doctor's supervision. Ideally, stress and the resulting anxiety should be dealt with without drugs.

Marijuana, cocaine, and heroin are the most popular drugs among the inmate population—often, that is why they are involved with the criminal justice system in the first place. But correctional workers sometimes turn to these drugs to cope with their lives. Marijuana is popular because it produces a feeling of "euphoria" and mellow well-being. Cocaine is popular because it results in a high of "energy." Heroin also helps relax its users by producing a euphoric feeling.

Drug use among corrections professionals has been documented in several states, as well as in the District of Columbia (American Correctional Association, 2003b). Many states now test job applicants and staff for drug use. The fallout from correctional workers' drug abuse is serious. Not only are families and friends affected by a drug-addicted worker's moods and behavior, but colleagues and inmates also are affected. Safety issues arise: How can a straight and sober worker depend on a coworker who is high or drunk?

Lack of Exercise

In 1993, the Centers for Disease Control reported that more Americans need to get more active. Research indicates that nearly 60 percent of Americans are completely or irregularly inactive. Researchers examined more than 1.1 million deaths in 1986 from nine key chronic illnesses, including stroke; heart disease; chronic obstructive pulmonary (lung) disease; liver disease; and lung, breast, cervical, and colorectal cancers. Significant, poor-health risk factors, such as smoking, high cholesterol, high blood pressure, obesity, and a sedentary lifestyle played a large part in these deaths (Squires, 1987). For example, smoking contributed to 32.8 percent of the deaths, and lack of exercise was a factor in 23.3 percent of the fatalities. Research released by the U.S. Centers for Disease Control (CDC) in 2003 stated that 120 million Americans are overweight, 10 percent do nothing in the way of exercise, and 16 percent do very little. At least thirty minutes of moderate activity most days of the week is recommended (Hellmich, 2003). In the twenty-first century, stress researchers are continuing to call for exercise to be a priority in our daily lives.

Exercise has many benefits. Aerobic exercise, such as walking and swimming, benefits the heart and lungs. Weight training builds strength and endurance. These benefits are important in maintaining the body's supply of adaptive energy. However, many correctional workers do not exercise regularly. This, when combined with a high-fat diet, can result in a body and mind that is out of shape and not prepared to deal with stress. Exercising energizes the body and mind. Thus, workers who do not exercise may fall into a "rut" of lethargy and fatigue. Exercise can reduce tension, anxiety, and mild depression (Whittlesey, 1986).

Exercise helps us get rid of tension. After a rough day dealing with offenders, workers can come home full of tension or frustration, which exercise can help release. One juvenile counselor says doing yard work helps him because the activity, sunshine and fresh air, and sense of accomplishment calms him down after a long day working with juveniles.

Correctional workers may quit smoking, use alcohol in moderation, and watch what they eat, but having an exercise regimen can be the most beneficial of all. The good feelings from an exercise program result not only in an increased ability to withstand stress, but also in a positive self-image. How we feel about ourselves affects our work. Correctional workers deal with offenders constantly. These offenders are always on the lookout for weaknesses to manipulate. Correctional workers should see, when they look at themselves in the mirror, a person who looks good, feels good, exhibits confidence, and commands respect. In a job where the worker must have self-confidence in his or her abilities and decisions, a positive self-image is a must.

Benefits from Exercise

People are often surprised by how good exercising makes them feel. Exercise energizes us. It gives us a chance to recharge our adaptive energy—the energy we need most when we are under stress. The following are just some of the benefits gained from a regular exercise program:

- muscles become firm
- heart and lungs strengthen
- weight is controlled
- blood pressure lowers
- sleep improves
- tension is released
- bones strengthen
- joints limber up
- appearance improves
- poise and presence of mind expands
- alertness increases
- energy levels are boosted

- confidence and self-esteem increase

- adaptive energy increases

Recent studies indicate that regular exercise, whether rigorous or mild, promotes wellness and helps us to be healthy enough to effectively manage stress. It can build up the body's hardiness to withstand the effects of continuous stress in corrections.

So, why do we not exercise more, especially in a job where we must be physically in shape and mentally alert? According to Barbara A. Brehm, Ed.D, professor of exercise and sports studies at Smith College, Northampton, Massachusetts:

- We *need* physical activity to stay healthy. If we are not physically active, muscles, joints and bones weaken. We accumulate fat, and our metabolic rate slows. Both blood sugar and blood pressure rise. Due to fat deposits collecting on artery walls, the blood supply to the heart, brain, kidneys, and other vital organs is reduced. While activities such as housework and gardening give us some activity, they are not real workouts. We should exercise regularly. Being inactive and sedentary may damage your health as much as smoking.

- Some people have trouble getting started. It may take reprioritizing and rescheduling our routines, because exercise has been "programmed" out of our hectic, "on the go" lifestyles.

- Lack of information is not an excuse. We should get information from recreation centers, gyms, and so forth. Agency health clinics that perform annual medical exams and local colleges that have physical education programs and staff also could provide seminars and training.

- Lack of time is not an excuse. Life can be rushed and pressured, but exercise can be put into daily routines: walking or cycling to work, doing at least thirty minutes of exercise a day, and so on. Maybe something in your life will have to be discontinued or put on hold to get exercise in. Health should be a priority. Dr. Brehm asks: If we are forced to make time for ourselves when we are sick (like calling in sick when we are ill), then why not make time for it now—to avoid getting sick?

(Brehm, 2002)

Positive coping, both physically and mentally, can result in a positive self-image. By coping through negative strategies, the image in the mirror will be one of an overweight, sloppy individual who does not look or feel good. If workers are not healthy, in shape, and drug free, they may start to feel depressed or despondent, further limiting their self-confidence. Another way to look at coping is this:

Stress can wear you out. When you feel worn out, you do not feel good at all. Life is tough enough, especially in a corrections career. Do what you can by positively coping to feel better.

Making Choices

You have a choice to have a positive self-image or a negative self-image. It takes time and effort to develop a positive self-image. In a job filled with negatives, correctional workers must take conscious steps to develop a frame of mind, in which they think they are worthy individuals with good qualities, abilities, and ideas.

Mental Coping

Correctional workers under stress must try to cope with thoughts, attitudes, and feelings. We do things to feel better physically (physical coping), and we adopt behaviors to deal with stress mentally. Just as some physical-coping strategies can be harmful, some mental habits can do more harm than good. Harmful mental strategies include suppressing feelings, generalizing or stereotyping, denying, projecting, rationalizing, and getting angry (Cheek, 1984).

Negative thoughts must be counteracted by positive thoughts and actions. You should concentrate on the positive aspects of work, rather than get into a negative rut. This can be accomplished by countering every negative thought with a positive thought. The inmate anger-management program: *Cage Your Rage* by Murray Cullen and the newer *Cage Your Rage for Women* by Judith Urquhart and Murray Cullen may offer staff some helpful tips in handling their own anger.

Suppressing Feelings

Correctional workers often keep their feelings locked inside them when they become angry, depressed, or tired from the stress. This reaction does not benefit anyone close to the worker and, in fact, can end up hurting everyone. These feelings eventually will explode outward at anyone in the way. Workers in this mode often identify with television or movie heroes—tough, stern, and strong. They think, "I'm tough, nothing bothers me." They believe that if they show how stress affects them, they will be weak. So, they keep it in. The result is poor relationships with others, coldness, silence, and pent-up anger. They are running from stress.

When You Think:	Say to Yourself:
This job is worthless.	This job is important to the criminal justice system and the public.
These offenders do not want my help.	I'll have to concentrate on the ones who do want help.
I look and feel terrible. It's because of the job.	I am responsible for the way I look and feel. I'll do something about it.
I'll never go anywhere in this job.	I should get training and better myself.
This job has too many hassles.	I'll do the best I can and take one day at a time.

For the past few months, Adrienne has felt despondent about her job. The constant noise and the demanding inmates are really getting to her. However, she refuses to let the stress get to her and promises herself that she will keep her mouth shut and just do her job. She talks to no one about her feelings or her stress. She just wants to be left alone. One day, after a long, hectic shift, Adrienne comes home, turns on the television before saying hello, opens a beer, and just sits and stares. Her husband tries to ask about her day. As their two children start to play in front of the television, the dog starts barking. Her husband asks several times what is wrong, but each time gets only silence as an answer. Finally Adrienne jumps up and yells, "Nothing is wrong. Just get the hell out of here and leave me alone." The family backs off, the children are in tears, and Adrienne returns to the television and her silence. The household atmosphere in a situation such as this is quite tense. Family members may begin avoiding the stressed-out person. In intimate relationships, communications and sexual activity may decrease, compounding the level of stress.

Generalizing and Stereotyping

The worker "lumps" people into categories based on generalizations, such as "all offenders are manipulators," "all volunteers are 'bleeding hearts,'" "all drug counselors believe everything the inmates say," and "supervisors are all alike—they never listen to us."

This "fight reaction" is an unrealistic way of viewing things. Workers with such opinions treat people accordingly, causing much friction in the workplace.

Denying

Many workers deny that stress even exists. They may give stress different names, such as pressure or heavy responsibilities, but it does not change the fact that they are experiencing stress. Denying stress is another flight technique.

Projecting

One common method for dealing with stress is projecting or passing the responsibility for it onto the system. For example, workers who say, "I feel lousy, it's the jail" do not realize they themselves can control how stress affects them. Overtime is a good example. Officers or probation officers who work overtime and feel burned out often blame supervisors, the courts, or the workload and fail to realize that the amount of overtime they work could be decreased or their time managed more effectively.

Rationalizing

Another common reaction to too much stress is to make up excuses for or rationalize problems resulting from stress. For example, one probation officer knows he and his wife never go out to dinner anymore, but blames it on his workload, which makes him tired. In reality, he is not doing anything to get reenergized. A juvenile counselor takes an antacid, but blames her stomach discomfort on a chili dog lunch, when, in reality, job pressures cause her stomach discomfort every day.

Anger

Anger is a common "fight" technique to mentally battle the things that cause stress. Effective correctional workers manage their anger. Although it may feel good at times to snap at people or yell at offenders, angry outbursts do more harm than good. Workers who are angry alienate colleagues, family members, and offenders.

In the last few years, angry behavior has emerged more frequently. Consider these examples (Peterson, 2000):

- Two shoppers in a Connecticut supermarket line engage in a fistfight over who should be first in newly opened checkout line.

- In Massachusetts, two fathers argue over rough play at their sons' hockey practice. One beats the other father to death.

- In Florida, a high school baseball coach faces charges that he broke an umpire's jaw after a disputed call.

Let's not forget these (Hales, 2001):

- A former fifty-one year old police officer turned salesman grabbed a golf club and almost beat up the driver in front of him because he slammed on his brakes. Luckily, he admits, he snapped out of it and drove away.

- A man from the Midwest would get so angry that he smashed up his lawn mower and tore off its wheels because it would not start. When golfing, he would have someone pick up his clubs, which he threw fifty-feet away.

Ever go out to eat? (Sagon, 2001):

- In two separate incidents in different Washington DC restaurants, a man was asked to have a seat in the bar while the hostess found a table for him. The man went into the restroom and slashed a painting with a pocketknife. In another establishment, a customer complained that the French fries were too soggy. The chef put them in the fryer for a few minutes, and then the customer complained that they were too crispy, threw them in the chef's face and stormed out.

What is the cause of these angry outbursts? Why can't people be more rational when handling stress? Some researchers say that more of us feel that things should go "our way." Other factors thrown into the mix include too little time, overcrowding (traffic, crowds, and so forth), technology, and demands for change (Peterson, 2000).

A key word describing this behavior is "rage." It is road rage when drivers on highways argue, and run each other off the road. Raging parents lose control at their children's sporting events, airplane passengers rage at the flight crew, or drivers fight over a parking space. One jail officer told the author that he made it a point to get to his son's Little League games as much as possible considering his schedule and shift work. He remembers seeing the parents losing control and yelling hysterically at coaches and umpires. He remembers thinking that the kids acted more maturely than the parents, and some inmates would not even act like that.

Dealing with Anger

It is important to understand that anger is natural, that everyone experiences anger, and that anger is a powerful emotion. When we are angry, we become energized. For example, a probation officer becomes angry with her supervisor for what she feels is an unjust criticism of a presentence report. As soon as the probation officer returns to her desk, she feels a burst of energy as she sits down to rewrite the report. Or a secretary in a jail records office becomes frustrated when files cannot be located because staff members are using them in other offices. Still angry, she goes to her desk and jots down a memo about the problem. She then types up the memo outlining a new-file checkout system. Angry? Yes, but in both cases, anger motivated the workers to accomplish positive things.

Anger is a "fight" response and an attempt to mentally cope with stress by lashing out. But handling stress by becoming angry and fighting the stress can negatively affect our health. Research has shown that anger is a "ready" condition. When we are angry, we are ready for whatever is coming. During rage and anger, the body secretes more adrenaline, more sugar is released, and more blood is pumped to the brain and muscles.

Too much anger or frequent anger that is not handled effectively can result in health problems, such as increased blood pressure and heart disease. Relationships can suffer, too, as angry workers lash out at those around them. We cannot avoid anger in our lives, but we must learn to deal with it in ways that make us winners, not losers.

According to Dr. Redford Williams, a psychiatry professor at Duke University, anger can be very destructive. Williams says that anger "sends your blood pressure sky-rocketing. It provokes your body to create unhealthy chemicals. For hostile people, anger is poison" (Ubell, 1990).

If you believe that anger is good to let out once in a while and it is not harmful, remember that anger is like a built-up dam of emotions that overflows. Tension, disillusionment, boredom, and frustration can fester, build up, and finally explode. In training, law enforcement professionals, including correctional workers, are told to act professionally, be strong, command respect, and above all, keep composed. But we do lose our composure, angrily at times, both at work and at home.

Psychologists say we can deal with anger in three ways (Glock, 1993):

- **venting:** screaming, yelling, or snapping at people
- **turning anger inward:** telling yourself it is your fault that you are angry
- **cooling down:** reflecting calmly on the situation

The key to managing anger is to keep calm. For example, Dave is a counselor in a work-release center. He has had a very busy and tiring day. He has arranged an interview for an offender, Tom, with a substance-abuse counselor. Tom is late, and the substance-abuse counselor is growing impatient. Dave can do any of the following things:

- start complaining loudly about worthless offenders and how they do not care (venting)

- keep his growing anger held in and tell himself he should have called Tom and reminded him about the meeting (turning anger inward)

- calm down and realize that the responsibility to be at the meeting rests with Tom, who was advised of the appointment three days earlier (cooling down)

The logical choice is the last one—calming down in order to think clearly. There are many benefits to being calm instead of holding in anger. In one study, healthy men who had high levels of hostility at age twenty-five were up to seven times more likely to get heart disease or die by the time they reached age fifty (Ubell, 1990). Other research shows that hostility and anger can "spur" the release of epinephrine, a hormone that makes the heart beat faster and blood pressure rise. This process can damage arteries, and eventually may cause a heart attack (Ubell, 1990). In 1986, a study at the University of Michigan concluded that people who regularly hold in or suppress their anger were more than twice as likely to die in the next twelve years as opposed to people who both recognize and express angry feelings (Glock, 1993).

Correctional workers must find ways to deal with anger—to express feelings (in positive, nonharmful ways) or to expend the energy that anger builds up. Although anger sometimes can motivate, over a long period, it also can be draining. According to Cheryl Sacra, a health writer "getting angry can sap your strength even more than spending the day cleaning your house or running an entire marathon"(1993). Correctional workers must change the way they manage themselves when stress leads to anger.

One way to manage anger is not to practice what is called "anger diversion," or more simply suppressing it— pretending it is not there. Some feel the physical effects of suppressing their anger such as tightness in the chest, shoulders, back, neck, or stomach. Others say that suppressing anger leads them to overeat or drink too much in an effort to soothe themselves. Some people decide not to be angry, but end up dealing with life through clenched teeth. Finally, some of us externalize anger by exploding outward, and this results in insulting and abusing others. These "others" can be coworkers, inmates, clients, friends, or loved ones. Anger diversion is counterproductive (Cox, 2001).

The opposite of anger diversion is assertive anger expression. This is when we are forced through positive coping to use and express anger in a positive, conscious, and deliberate way. We get it out without anyone getting in the "line of fire." The buildup of stress is prevented, the negative effects of stress are countermanded, and our relationship with others and our self-respect are protected (Cox, 2001).

How to Manage Your Anger

The following steps can help you to both be aware of your anger and deal with it in constructive ways.

1. *Use "angry energy" in constructive ways.* If you come home from work angry, but full of energy, do something that needs doing: vacuum, clean the closets, or mow the lawn. If you want something fun, exercise instead. Shoot some baskets, walk or jog around a neighborhood park, or run through an aerobic-exercise routine. Work out the tension.

2. *Practice distraction.* If an offender is late for an appointment, distract yourself from the problem by listening to the radio, calling a friend, or just getting out of the office for a few minutes. One worker kept magazines nearby and would take one to two minutes to glance at an article—a simple distraction to take the "edge" off.

3. *Play with pets.* Playing with a dog, cat, or another pet can calm you down and take your mind off your anger. At the end of a hard day, it is nice to come home to a loving pet.

4. *Change your habits.* If you "jump" into situations too fast or are always willing to lend a hand, you may be overwhelming yourself. Say "no" more often. Do not take on too much.

5. *Forgive those who anger you.* Perhaps you and an inmate had words. Do not hold a grudge. The same goes for coworkers and family.

6. *Discuss your anger with friends or loved ones.* You even may want to talk to the person who made you angry in the first place. But first, wait until you are calm. Talk to your spouse or friends about your anger. You may receive good advice and support on how to calm down. Some researchers advocate the cultivation of an "anger buddy" (Cox, 2001). An anger buddy is a friend or loved one with whom you make a pact to listen to each other about what angers each of you, without trying to fix, pacify, or explain the angry feelings away. Keep your anger buddy's phone number or e-mail address handy.

7. *Relax.* Take deep breaths, calm down, and practice the relaxation techniques that are discussed in Chapter 8.

8. *Keep a written journal* (Cox, 2001). For at least a week, write down all of the things that irritate you, or make you frustrated, resentful, or jealous. This includes all forms of anger. Review it regularly, noting what you did or did not do about

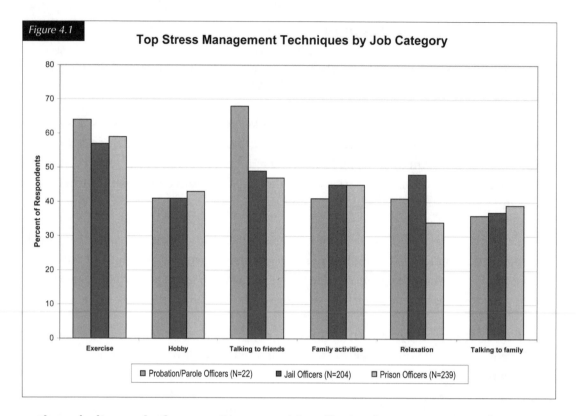

Figure 4.1

Top Stress Management Techniques by Job Category

□ Probation/Parole Officers (N=22)   ■ Jail Officers (N=204)   □ Prison Officers (N=239)

these feelings, whether negative or positive. Try to do more positive things. You also can keep an anger calendar and mark an X when you are angry. It will show you how often anger controls you. In a related sense, see what your "hot buttons" are. What makes you angry? Can you deal with these issues in a better way? What are the real issues—trouble at home, conflict with your supervisor? Deal with them in a positive way. (Hales, 2001).

9. *Use an anger "mantra" or slogan.* Try words such as "I will not get angry, I will not blow my top." This may require that you say those words a lot at first, but it works (Hales, 2001).

10. *Keep emotions in control and avoid "name calling"* (Hales, 2001). Name calling is unprofessional and rude, and once those words leave our mouths, we cannot take them back

Coping at Work and at Home

In the survey (*see* Chapter 3) the author conducted, probation and parole officers, jail officers, and prison officers rated their stress levels on duty and off duty. As seen by Figure 4.1, most (more than 50 percent) reported medium stress on duty. In the next category, most of the jail and prison officers indicated low levels of off-duty stress, while the probation and parole officers reported low-to-medium levels of stress. The difference may be the caseloads, seeing offenders in the field, overtime, and so forth.

Coping at work and at home means changing the way we deal with stress on and off the job. Coping at work can take many forms. Changing a mid-afternoon snack from a bag of chips to an apple is better health-wise. Taking more breaks from your desk benefits your mind and recharges your energy level. Cutting down on coffee is beneficial. Other coping methods include reorganizing your work station, talking more to coworkers, saying "no" more often to offenders, playing relaxing music in your office, and signing up for training.

In the author's survey, corrections staff reported the six top stress-management techniques:

- exercising
- engaging in a hobby
- talking to friends
- participating in family activities
- relaxing
- talking to family

Two top-coping techniques for both physical and mental health were clearly reported: exercising and talking to friends. These are beneficial in reducing the stress of corrections.

Please *see* Appendix C for more ways to cope with stress. Learning to cope does not have to cost anything but your time and effort. The negative effects of stress—anger, tension, and fatigue—must be counteracted by simple things we can do on the job. The possibilities are endless. All it takes is commitment, a desire to feel better, and a little effort.

If you carry the weight of your stress home everyday, then positive coping at home is a must. For example, the anger and tension that has built up all day should not spill over to your family. Coping at home, like coping at work, means doing positive things when under stress to benefit the body and mind. At home you could take a walk, go out to a movie, rent a video and have a "movie night," ask the children about school, take a nap, work in the yard, or cook a special meal. Try not to talk about work all the time.

Listening is important to reducing the negative effects of stress at home. Remember to listen to your spouse and children—they too have their own stressors. Beware of being so wrapped up in your job that you end up tuning your family out when they need to talk to you. Coping at home means to get involved with home matters. Part of this is to care for your home, to keep it clean and uncluttered, and make it your refuge from stress. It also is important to do fun activities with the people who share your home and are a big part of your life.

Balance

We hear a lot about putting balance into our life. Positive coping can do that, because so many aspects of life can be balanced if we learn to handle stress the right way. Imagine yourself in a rowboat on a quiet lake. Pretend that the boats going by you are stressors, and feel how the boat rocks as you encounter their wakes. You know that the boat has to be put back on an even keel—it must be balanced.

After reading this chapter, stop and take a self-inventory (Albrecht, 1999) about the balance in your life:

- **Physical Health:**   *How is your general health?*

    Do you have energy and stamina?
    Do you feel ill or sick frequently?
    Do you feel pain frequently?
    Do you mask pain and illness by using caffeine, nicotine, drugs and/or alcohol?

- **Mental Health:**   *What is your overall attitude toward life, negative or positive?*

    Most of the time, are you happy and content?
    Do you frequently feel anger, fear, apprehension, and anxiety?

- **Family Relationships:**   *Do you have strong bonds with your immediate family?*

    In your home, do you feel happy and safe?
    Do the people closest to you provide love, support, and a "cushion" from the outside world?

- **Love Relationships:** *Are you in a loving relationship with someone who makes you feel content?*

   Does this person make you feel better about yourself, especially when you are stressed out?

- **Professional Life:** *Are you happy in your career choice or job?*

   Are you happy in your current position or is it time for a change?

   Are you able to grow in your job, both personally and professionally

   Do you like going to work?

   Do you like the majority of the tasks that you have to do?

   Do you get along well with your peers, supervisors, inmates, and clients?

   When you supervise and direct subordinates, do you do it with a sense of pride?

- **Social Relationships:** *Do you have several close friends on whom you can rely?*

   Are you able to share your thoughts and feelings with them?

   Are you able to make friends easily and establish social relationships on various levels, including with people outside of corrections?

Balance is a key factor in stress reduction. In the areas listed above, if positive coping techniques, such as exercise and anger management are major parts of our lives, then these areas: physical and mental health, relationships with others, and our professional life will stay balanced and not be off center. Attention and energy devoted to these areas will pay off by making our professional lives more fulfilling. Your corrections job, like any other job, should not be the central focus of your life. There are other things in life. We should work to live our lives to their fullest potential, not live to work (Albrecht, 1999).

Humor can be a very effective stress-reducing tool. Laughing, even smiling, often benefits both our bodies and minds. According to the Mayo Clinic, laughter relaxes the skeletal muscles of your arms and legs, and provides good exercise for the heart by raising the heart rate. Humor and laughter release pent-up feelings such as frustration and anger. They also can lessen pain and help breathing. Some hospitals provide patients with humor libraries, clowns, and nurses who crack jokes. Humor—a joke, the squad "clown," a funny movie, and so forth, all can help us positively cope with stress. Laugh—you will feel better (www.mayoclinic.com). One jail classification officer likes humor in the workplace: *"After you interview and deal with drug addicts, sex offenders, and the mentally ill, it is refreshing for coworkers to laugh, poke fun at one another, and just goof around a little bit. Everyone feels better."*

Appendix C offers numerous suggestions on ways to cope at home and at work. As you learn about various healthy coping methods, explore them so that you can develop a plan that works for you.

Communicating without Stress

After reading this chapter, you should understand the following:

- How to communicate with others to avoid undue stress

- How to be assertive in a positive way both at work and at home

- How to use good communication skills for avoiding manipulation and conflict, and for listening

In the field of corrections, a lot depends on communication, whether you are a probation officer filing a presentence report or a jail officer sharing information about inmates at the end of your shift. On or off the job, much of our daily life depends on what we say to people and how we say it. Just as important is written communication—how we put information on paper. Knowing and practicing good communication skills can reduce the number of stressors we encounter. Communicating properly also is a way of positively coping with stress.

Communication is the exchange of information about our ideas, feelings, opinions, and observations. It is also an exchange of factual information. People cannot function in today's society without good communication skills. We must let others know, by verbal or written communication, our position on situations. We also must be able to listen to others.

In corrections, good communication skills are crucial. As correctional workers, the majority of our time is spent verbally communicating with offenders, clients, colleagues, supervisors, and the courts. Correctional workers, as a rule, must try not to let the effects of stress hamper communication with others.

Unfortunately, we often forget to extend the same courtesy we offer our professional colleagues to our loved ones at home. Communication at home often takes the form of "half listening" and we feel freer to be ourselves, which often means being silent, cold, nasty, and sarcastic.

It is important, too, to look at our appearance and how we act. "Dress for success" is not a cliché, as many people judge how successful a person is by how well groomed he or she is. Good straightforward eye contact is crucial, so is facial expression. The face shows six primary emotions: fear, anger, distrust, surprise, happiness, or sadness (Pfeiffer and Webster, 1992). Try to keep a positive face or at least a "poker face," which is neutral and will not add stress to the conversation. However, "happiness faces" are permitted in appropriate situations.

What Is Communication?

Communication in its most basic form consists of a message sender, the message (or information), and the receiver. By sending and receiving messages, we interact with others. This is called interpersonal communications. According to the American Correctional Association's training course, "Interpersonal communication is the way we interact, the way we get along, the way we build and maintain ongoing relationships with others" (1986). The key word is "way." How well we get along depends on the way we communicate, and that depends on how we handle stress.

Verbal Communication Skills

To communicate in a positive way, workers must be aware of the fundamentals of good communication. According to the Interpersonal Communication (IPC) model of communication, which is taught widely throughout the corrections field, there are four basic tenets to practice: positioning, posturing, observing, and listening. How stress is being handled can directly affect how these four tenets are practiced.

Positioning

Positioning means taking the best position to see and hear the person or persons communicating with you. By now, however, you probably have developed a number of positioning habits, which you need to become aware of and then evaluate.

Good positioning requires that you face the person you are talking to squarely and put a proper distance between you and this person. For offenders, this may be two-to-three feet, closer for friends and loved ones. Good positioning will help you feel in control, while at the same time, make the other person feel you are paying attention.

Bad positioning occurs when you are sideways to the other person, have your back turned, or are placed in an awkward, indirect position to the person with whom you are trying to communicate. Bad positioning can cause stress. The person talking to you will feel insignificant, ignored, and unimportant. If you are badly positioned while talking to an inmate, the inmate may become frustrated. If you are at home, your loved one may feel unimportant and frustrated if you are not properly positioned. Their stress level may go up and an argument may result.

Posturing

By using your body effectively, you can assume a posture that shows the other person you are interested in the message, are in control, are confident, and have strength. How you move and hold yourself has developed over your lifetime. Some of what you do naturally is good. Some may be ineffective. You will need to be more aware of how you use your body when you communicate.

Good posturing means standing erect, not displaying habits that bother the person you are talking to, avoiding barriers (desks, tables) between you and the other person, and leaning toward the other person, and making eye contact. Good posturing minimizes feelings of stress because your body says, "I am interested in you." Good, clear eye contact is especially important when communicating with offenders, because it makes it psychologically harder for them to lie or to manipulate you (although that does not mean they will not try or that it will not happen). At home, good posturing helps, too. You will be surprised how much conflict can be avoided by using good posturing. If you are looking around the room or away from someone talking to you, that person will not believe you are listening or that you care.

Bad posturing is slouching, leaning back, looking off in the distance, or fidgeting. Poor posturing sends the nonverbal message of "who cares?" On the job, offenders become angry. At home, loved ones may feel rejected.

Another aspect of posturing is distance. For a public space, twelve to twenty-five feet away from another person is permissible. At this distance, you are not crowding anyone. A good rule for a social distance is four-to-twelve feet. You are still communicating, but at a respectful distance. If you want a personal conversation that shows sincerity toward the other person, whether at home or at work, standing eighteen inches to four feet is all right. Finally, for an intimate conversation, the appropriate distance is eighteen inches or less. You may want to measure out these distances when you are alone so you understand what this distance really means. Then, when you are engaged in conversation, you can judge if the distance is appropriate. Consider the type of conversation or communication that is to take place. Respect the other person's space. If you invade it and get too close, it may cause the other individual undue stress (Pfeiffer and Webster, 1992). Think how you would feel.

Observing

Observing means looking at the persons you are communicating with during the whole conversation to see if they are concerned with anything. Are the individuals nervous or apprehensive? Are they listening? You can look for clues in the way individuals hold themselves to determine if they understand you or if they are interested Also, observing includes checking out the environment (surroundings) in which you are interacting.

Good observation skills require that you are taking the surroundings into account. This is important if you are communicating in quiet, private surroundings, especially if the information exchanged is confidential or sensitive. Noisy environments at work and at home can make even the simplest conversation stressful.

Bad observation skills indicate that you do not care where you are or if the message is understood. A burned-out jail officer is writing his log when an upset inmate approaches. The inmate says he is having a personal problem and needs to talk with someone. The officer, without looking up or putting his pen down, says, "You are not the only one with problems, but alright, tell me about it." While the inmate talks about his impending divorce and how depressed he feels, the officer continues writing in his log. He does not ask the inmate to sit down and does not try to establish eye contact with the inmate. If the officer took some time to observe the inmate, he would realize the inmate is under severe stress, which could lead to an emotional breakdown, acting out, or suicide. Or the same worker may go home and try to talk to his wife about something that is bothering him while the children are playing and the television is blaring. Criticizing inmates and staff in front of other inmates and staff is another example of poor observation skills in communication. It indicates that the person speaking is unconcerned about what is being said, where they are, and who is listening.

Listening

Effective listening is an art. It is the ability to really understand what the other's message is. Often, listening is more important than speaking.

Good listening skills include the ability to "detach yourself" from distractions and concentrate on the message. For example, you come home after a stressful day, and you have a lot on your mind. Your daughter received a bad grade at school and is crying. She needs to talk to you about it. You need to put your concerns aside, lean forward, and listen to her. By doing so, her stress is decreased.

Bad listening skills include not listening, not facing the person, not making eye contact, interrupting, "half listening," and engaging in distracting behavior. Distracting behavior includes talking to someone on the phone while someone is present and talking, and displaying nervous habits, such as clicking a pen, for example. As one veteran jail officer said:

"The best coworkers and supervisors I have worked with were ones who did not answer the phone and let the machine get the message, did not look at the computer screen, and turned and focused on me. The worst ones were those who let interruptions occur, checked and answered e-mail, and half-faced me. At home, I learned that when my wife has had a bad day and really needs to vent or talk, I turn off the television, shoo the kids away, and face her, look her in the eye, and listen. I guess that it is due to all of the years that I dealt with negative, bad listeners."

By using poor listening skills, you are telling the other person that you simply are not hearing the message—you do not care. If, when your daughter is trying to explain her bad grade, you turn on the television, nod at her, and say "uh-huh," you will upset her more. If an offender is trying to talk to you and you are half listening or interrupting, you will increase the offender's tension.

Here are some ideas that you can use to improve your listening skills (Pfeiffer and Webster, 1992):

- Listen to the total message. Try to understand what is not being said: Nonverbal clues such as inflection, hesitancy, and body language are important. Up to 65 percent of a message is sent to the recipient without words.

- Avoid letting your own emotions and opinions cloud the message. Keep your emotions under control.

- Focus on the message—what is being said, rather than what the person looks like.

- Try to avoid having the last word. The other person may have valid points and may be right. If you interrupt and feel that you must dominate the conversation and have the last word, you may miss the message. As one correctional officer relates:

"I had to learn not to interrupt, both on the job and at home. My wife told me that I always jump into our conversations before she is finished talking. My sergeant always used to say, 'LISTEN.' It is when I saw it on my evaluations and my

supervisor told me that I figured I had to get this bad habit under control. Now I sort of 'shut up.' I'll have my chance to talk."

- Mentally summarize what is being said. We can think about four times as fast as the average person can speak. The average person can speak about 125 words per minute. Summarize in your mind what is being said and filter out what you can use.

- Evaluate what you hear and do not take everything at face value.

- Paraphrase the message—put it in your own words.

- Clarify: Ask questions for both understanding and for more information.

- Provide feedback. Share your thoughts with the speaker as a result of understanding the message.

Written Communication Skills

Learning to communicate effectively in writing can help relieve stress on the job. Many correctional workers become frustrated because information either is not received in writing or is poorly written and leaves out important details.

What is needed is a "commonsense" approach to written communications. It is frustrating to go to a file or memorandum book, for example, and find that important information has not been included. Illegible entries on an inmate's classification file could be life threatening.

Correctional workers should ask themselves: "Would I like to receive my own written communications?" With this in mind, the following are some guidelines for stress-free written communication:

1. **Write legibly.** If you are making an entry into a case file, write clearly so everyone using the file can read the information. Look at your handwriting. Do you tend to scrawl? If so, you may have to print or type your entry. Make memos or notes clear and legible.

2. **Include all information.** In training academies, correctional officers are taught to include who, what, when, where, how, why (if known), and the action taken. Write memos and file entries the same way. Do not rush. Many correctional workers pride themselves on the fact that they can sit down at a typewriter or word processor and "bang out" a report or memo quickly. This is good if all information is included. It is stressful and embarrassing to discover later that some facts were left out of a report or file entry. If you compose as you type, have a checklist of things to include. Do not rely solely on memory.

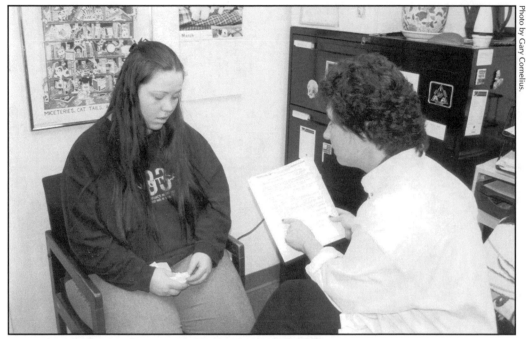

Photo by Gary Cornelius.

Informing a probationer of news, such as being violated and returning to jail, can put a probation/parole officer under stress.

3. **Include all "players."** When writing information, ensure it is distributed or passed on to all staff members who need to know it or who can use it. For example, if a supervisor puts out a memo changing the times of the jail head counts, naturally the confinement staff will get copies. However, other sections also need the information: classification because they call inmates down to the offices, maintenance because they go onto the floors for repairs, and the entrance/control booth to control visits.

In summary, if information is clearly presented, unnecessary questions and confusion are avoided and so is stress.

Communication and Offender Manipulation

Offender "con games" and manipulation are definitive stressors in corrections work. Being played for a fool by offenders can cause frustration, anger, and a loss of self-esteem. No correctional worker enjoys being controlled by offenders. Offenders can be superb actors who can concoct stories, falsehoods, and lies to have staff do their bidding. An offender's goal is not only to be in control of the situation (whether under supervision or incarcerated), but to be comfortable, as well.

Correctional workers can guard against manipulation by taking the following steps:

1. **Get educated.** Go to seminars on offender manipulation. Read everything you can about the offenders' culture, behavior, actions, and manipulation.

Photo by Gary Cornelius

Dealing with impatient and rude citizens and clients can be a major stressor.

2. **Know policies and procedures.** Know the agency's policies and procedures, not just the general orders, but also the informal guidelines and directives. All correctional workers should know their jobs thoroughly and better than the offender.

3. **Say no.** For some correctional workers, this is difficult. One jail classification counselor had difficulty saying no to offenders and would stop whatever he was doing whenever an inmate knocked on his office door. Subsequently, he would work long hours catching up on his work. Correctional workers must learn to say no to offenders when they make unreasonable requests, ask for favors that are against policies and procedures, or demand to see workers at inconvenient times.

4. **Know what is going on.** Workers should keep up with information about offenders in case files and institutional reports. Check things out before you give answers or make decisions. The exceptions are emergencies, but you should have enough information on hand to make a fast, proper decision.

5. **Practice stress management.** If you are stressed out over some things and it shows, offenders will be willing and able to "step right on in" to help you out. In other words, they become your new friends or support group, and they hope you will turn to them for comfort instead of your supervisors or peers. If you do, you may see them not as offenders, but as "nice" people who are willing to help. Of course, the cost is severe—breaking the rules, being conned into bringing in contraband, and so forth. A correctional staff person showing the following signs of burnout or heavy stress is showing "red flags" for the offender manipulator (Cornelius, 2001):

- exhaustion

- apathy toward his/her duties or the job

- inability to relax: being tense and wound up

- bitterness or sour attitude toward the job

- low morale

- constant complaining

- frequently impatient or easily frustrated

- frequently calls in sick or leaves work for the next person

- lack of interaction with coworkers: alone and out on a limb

Positive Assertiveness

Assertiveness includes stating your position, opinion, or the side of an issue that you are communicating to others. In other words, you get your side across without causing arguments, tension, or undue stress.

Correct assertiveness can be used on the job and at home. Correct assertiveness incorporates several commonsense approaches to good communication, such as keeping calm, putting yourself in the other's place, and looking at the whole situation. It means showing respect and consideration for other people (Cheek, 1984). Asserting yourself appropriately means considering the context, maintaining calm, considering another's point of view, explaining your side, coming to a solution, considering the consequences, and being consistent.

Consider the context. The surroundings of the situation must be considered. Do not try to talk seriously to a loved one, inmate, or staff member among noise, distractions, or visitors. Shut the door, turn off the television, ask the children to go outside, turn on the answering machine, and tell visitors you will get with them later. Do not criticize inmates or staff in front of others.

Maintain calm. Keep calm and relaxed when communicating with others. If the other person is tense, the last thing you should do is to display anger.

Consider other points of view. It is important to see the other side of the situation. Have the other person—no matter whom—explain his or her point of view. You may disagree, but at least you will be looked on as someone who will listen to another point of view and try to understand it.

Explain your side. Tell the other person how you perceive the situation. For example, an offender asks to be transferred to another cellblock. He says it is because his current cellblock is too noisy. You explain to him why you cannot transfer him for that reason and that it would make more work for the staff than is necessary. However, you tell the inmate you will ask the staff to advise the inmates to keep quiet. This explanation of the answer is better than just saying a curt, one-syllable "no." The inmate may not like the answer, but he will respect you for explaining it.

At home, this is important, too. If you are fatigued from stress at home and your spouse asks you to do something, do not just say "no," explain why. Perhaps you are not feeling well and just need a few hours to relax.

Come to a solution. Work with the other person to come to a solution. Ask the other person for suggestions about how to solve the problem. In cases of resistant offenders, one jail counselor simply says, "You have heard my side of this problem, and I have heard yours. These are your choices. . . ." This displays calm, direct assertiveness. Do not forget the importance of compromise.

For example, Kathy is a probation officer who makes field visits on Wednesdays. As a result, she usually arrives home late on those days. Kathy's daughter has just started a Wednesday afternoon ballet class. Kathy's husband, Joe, also could not take her every Wednesday due to his work conflicts. Kathy and Joe realized they would need to work out a compromise. Either one of them could have taken the burned-out approach and said, "I can't. Wednesdays are bad. That's the end of the discussion." Instead, Kathy said she would change her field day to another day of the week and that she would take her daughter every other Wednesday. Together, they agreed that Joe would talk to his supervisor about adjusting his hours. Another approach could have been to see if there was another, more convenient time the class was held or to get another parent to take her to class and then either Kathy or Joe would pick the girls up after class.

Consider the consequences. All of your actions have consequences, many of which are predictable. At home, if you communicate angrily and coldly and snap at others, the consequences will be a stressful personal life. While communicating with others, think about the results of the path you take. This applies to offenders, too. If you are talking about a course of action—a transfer or a presentence report—think of the results. Will they make your relationship better or worse?

Be consistent. Do not run hot and cold. With offenders, workers should not be angry one minute and calm the next. The same is true for personal relationships.

The people around you—offenders, coworkers, loved ones— never should have to be wary of you because you are moody, and your communication style changes.

By practicing positive assertiveness and good communication all the time—on and off the job—you will be on your way to a lifestyle with reduced stress that not only will enrich your life, but your family's as well.

Conflict

In all of our lives there is conflict, whether it is at work or at home. No one expects everyone to agree or do what we want all of the time. In conflict, you can assert yourself as described above, plus using these tips (Pfeiffer and Webster, 1992):

- **Take the first step:** You are feeling stressed out. Approach the other person and do not let the stress build up.

- **Schedule a meeting:** A calm, interruption-free atmosphere is important. The time to talk to your loved one or spouse is not when the kids are up and needing help with homework, or when one of you is leaving in a few minutes. At work, the same applies. A good rule is to meet in a comfortable, neutral setting, away from distractions, interruptions, and noise. It may mean going out for lunch, dinner, or for a walk. Find a quiet office and close the door. Put the phone on hold.

- **Get your anger under control:** Even if the other person is angry, that does not mean that you have to be. Listen, keep calm, respect his or her view, and let it be known that you are hearing the problem.

- **Keep the focus on the problem:** Keep personalities out of the conversation. Avoid blame, guilt, and punishment. Try to negotiate.

- **Keep the relationship adult:** At work, remember that you and the other person do not have to be friends, just professional coworkers. At home, do not act immature or childish. Remember, if you really love this person, act like an adult.

- **Be polite:** In conflict at work or at home, there is no room for rudeness. Be respectful.

- **Actively *listen*** to the other person.

How you communicate with others says two things: what kind of person you are—pushy, inattentive, distracted, or interested, caring, and sincere. The last three can reduce stress in communications. The other thing that is said is how mature you are. The mature person keeps his or her stress in check, and tries not to cause the other person undue stress.

Managing Employees Under Stress: New Strategies

After reading this chapter, you should understand the following:

• What contributes to an employee's stress

• How supervisors can decrease stress in their staff

• What supervisors can do to improve work conditions

• Why employee assistance programs are so important

• How to handle stress in the supervision of direct-supervision units

Perhaps one of the most difficult aspects of being a supervisor is dealing with employees under stress. In this respect, supervision is like a double-edged sword. Not only do the demands of the institution and offenders have to be met, but also meeting those demands is made harder when staff is under extreme stress. Managers and supervisors need to learn to manage employees effectively in a stressful workplace.

Clearly, in corrections, line staff complete the majority of the basic, bottom-line work. The men and women who work "in the trenches" conduct head counts, file court records, make inmate transfers, fix prison door locks, and see probationers and parolees. As the population of the correctional institutions and the caseloads of probation and parole officers increase, the line staff must meet the increasing needs and carry out the mission of the agency. It is the job of mid-level managers (for example, the section heads, probation/parole district supervisors, and sergeants) to see that the work gets done in the most efficient way possible.

The less stress staff members are under, the better they will perform. Staff members who work in harmony as a team generally get more done and feel better about their jobs. Research has indicated that workers who trust the people they work for, say they have a good workplace, have pride in their jobs, and enjoy the people with whom they work (Ayres and Flanagan, 1990).

Unfortunately, stress sometimes gets in the way. Workers who are under severe stress can impede their own good work and that of others. Managers, especially those who closely supervise employees in critical operations, must pay close attention to the level of stressors that affect workers in their areas of responsibility.

Supervisors must get the most and best work out of subordinates, but to do this, supervisors need to be aware of the physical and behavioral environment of the workplace. Observation skills are important. For example, a probation district supervisor must be aware of the physical layout of the workplace, including office space, file storage, and how many probation officers share offices. Behavioral aspects also are important. Are the probation officers getting along? Is the work completed correctly? Are workers abusing sick leave? How is morale?

As Larry Woodruff, the health promotion director for the Oregon Board on Public Safety, reported (1993), a 1986 study of 241 Alabama correctional officers indicated that 60 percent of those officers felt that inconsistent instruction from supervisors was a stressor. A second study of 364 Alabama correctional officers found that poor administrative practices, such as lack of clear guidelines, lack of crisis management, and rules that were inoperable, contributed significantly to job stress and burnout.

While the stressors encountered in corrections are discussed in detail in Chapter 3, supervisors must realize that the employee may be having a bad day at home or at work. For example, an argument with a spouse or significant other, illness, financial worries, and so forth, could come into play. Things at work may be getting to the employee and causing stress—not getting along with a colleague, working a rough post, or having a bad experience on the witness stand in court—all could be factors. Also, a supervisor should consider factors such as failing to get promoted, being denied a transfer request, or rejecting of an idea or suggestion that the employee may have submitted after spending a lot of time in research.

No workplace, office, or correctional institution is perfect. There always will be workers who are never satisfied. However, the average worker is no different from any other worker at any other job. He or she wants to earn a decent living, support a family, and move up the career ladder. The average worker will respond favorably to supervisors and managers who try to enhance the workplace by improving the physical plant and operations.

Photo by Gary Cornelius

One way to reduce stress is to talk to your colleagues. Share with them what is bothering you—it's better than holding it in.

Employee Stressors

Supervisors must understand the job stressors employees encounter. Law enforcement and correctional workers have identified the following stressors similar to those listed in Chapter 3 (Cheek 1984; Rensberger and Shine, 1989; Ayres and Flanagan, 1990; Pranzo and Pranzo, 1999):

- poor supervision
- lack of employee input into decisions and policy
- large amounts of paperwork
- conflict in roles and job functions
- vague ideas of goals and mission
- low morale
- lack of communication with management
- lack of training

- favoritism by the administration

- rules/decisions that are impractical and cannot be enforced

- quick, rapid changes in policies

- lack of feedback to ideas or administrators not being responsive

- a critical supervisor who is always a "nitpicker"

- work overload for too long: for example: frequent double shifts, overtime, "don't go home until it's done"

- lack of recognition, thanks, or praise

There is no formula, or rhyme or reason to what subordinates are going through when they knock on their supervisor's door and ask if they can come in and talk. Some staff are not bothered by work stressors, but may be having a bad time at home. The important thing to realize is that supervisors are to help staff and not just to manage work and give orders.

Supervisors Can Help Decrease Staff Stress

Supervisors can reduce stress by following three basic steps:

- controlling their own stress

- recognizing and helping stressed-out workers cope with their stress

- improving working conditions: enhancing the workplace

We will discuss each of these. Correctional workers look to their supervisors for direction, guidance, and support. Supervisors should guide workers through tasks, clarify priorities, and ensure mistakes are corrected. If workers are stressed out, productivity goes down. Supervisors should not add to this problem by being unproductive due to unmanaged stress. For example, if an officer is burning out and files an incident report on a serious event, such as a fight, the officer's boredom or irritability associated with burnout may cause him or her to do a sloppy job writing the report. The supervisor reviews the report for completeness and detail. If the supervisor is dissatisfied with her job due to stress, she may give the report only a cursory review before the report gets filed. A bad report that is not properly written, reviewed, or corrected may have repercussions down the line in an inmate lawsuit or criminal court actions.

Subordinates should not see a supervisor "take it out" on a staff member. This is one sure way to reduce morale. Supervisors should envision themselves as the captain who is calm on the bridge guiding the ship through stormy seas.

Many correctional workers aspire to get promoted, move upward, and work as supervisors and managers. But, when they do, their lives change. People who they worked with and perhaps associated with, as positive coping mechanisms, are now subordinates. Perhaps they used to complain about the agency's policies—now they have to support and implement them.

Consider this view concerning supervisors and stress management from John Carr, executive director of Rhode Island's Centurion Program, which provides stress management, counseling, and peer support to law enforcement and corrections staff:

"Within a paramilitary organization, as in any other grouping of professionals, [soldiers or line staff] aspire to become [officers or supervisors]. In the pyramid of a paramilitary law enforcement or department of corrections organization, as one rises in rank, while responsibility and visibility increase, one's peer support group and protection often decrease. At the same time, [soldiers] possess certain distinct advantages in terms of numbers, collegial support, union representation, and contractual protections.

"The first move into 'middle management' often provides for a unique set of stressors as the new correctional or law enforcement supervisor discovers. The price that one pays for advancements [is] that of former friendships and the need to 'prove' oneself to a new 'peer group' [upper management, or headquarters]. In our experience, it is crucial that the supervisor-administrator develop a set of supports both internal and external to his/her agency to balance the burdens associated with rank and responsibility.

"An administrator or [officer] is not going to stand [in] roll call and confide to the [soldiers] that he/she is clueless as to how to implement a new policy. The [officer] or administrator also is not going to confide to the chief political authority [such as the sheriff] that he/she has little confidence in a new program initiative. Top administrators often perceive that they become increasingly isolated from collegial support as they rise in rank."

Supervisors when they get promoted often go through the same stressors as the rank and file—when dealing with changes and new demands. The stress-coping techniques are just as important for supervisors as they are for line staff.

Not only do operations suffer because of stressed-out supervisors, but morale does, too. If supervisors issue conflicting orders, vague instructions, or take a "flight" outlook and isolate themselves from their subordinates, the morale of the staff will suffer. Line staff might say, "If the boss doesn't care, why should I?" A morale problem will surface with sloppy work, griping, and a general sense of mediocrity pervading the workplace.

Supervisors must learn to be in touch with their physical and mental well-being. Supervisors should take time to examine themselves in terms of how things are going in their personal and professional lives. Supervisory personnel must be educated in stress management through reading books, attending seminars, and taking advantage of other resources. They must realize that they can be "stress carriers" who have a direct effect on their staff. Gina, a department section head whose marriage is crumbling, must realize that the sick leave she has been taking leaves her section without her guidance and knowledge. Staff members who need to see her are frustrated because she spends a lot of time on the telephone arguing with her spouse. The last thing any workplace needs is a leader who cannot lead because he or she cannot manage stress.

Here are five good suggestions for supervisors concerning keeping control of their stress (Phillips and McConnell, 1996; Seiter, 2002):

- **Learn to say NO**, or at least speak up [respectfully] when the last request, demand, or directive from your superior finally becomes too much.

- **Do not let work pile up** until it becomes unmanageable and uncontrollable. You may end up "dumping" it on your staff, and they will resent it.

- **Delegate work** before it gets out of control.

- **Vary the pace.** Intersperse short, manageable, quiet tasks among the more stressful and hectic tasks.

- **Reduce the physical response to stress** by relaxing, stretching, deep breathing, or walking to clear your head.

Recognizing and Helping Stressed-out Workers Cope With Their Stress

Along with recognizing and managing their own stressors, supervisors must be on the lookout for employees who are suffering from unmanaged stress. More important, the supervisor must deal with these employees, who usually are salvageable.

The worst thing supervisors can do is to isolate themselves. It is easy to fall into this trap by staying in an office and only addressing issues and problems that find their way through your door. A supervisor who is interested in reducing stress is mobile and communicative with the staff. The following guidelines should be used to detect employees under stress:

1. **Watch employees for changes in personality and behavior.** Changes in a worker's personality or behavior (for example, a usually cheerful worker turning "sour") may indicate anger and frustration associated with burnout. Most people experience an occasional bad day. A worker who has bad days all the time may be experiencing burnout.

2. **Look for indicators of negative coping.** Do changes in behavior indicate negative coping? At a social function, a shift lieutenant notices that one of the officers on his squad, a moderate drinker, is drinking heavily. Another officer, who normally is a light smoker, is smoking heavily. These signs could indicate stress that they are not coping with positively.

3. **Listen for frequent negative comments.** Workers under stress frequently vocalize their frustrations.

4. **Be aware of a decline in the quality of work or in good work habits.** Preoccupation with stressors and mental or physical fatigue can lead to deteriorating work habits.

5. **Be alert for complaints of the physical signs of stress.** Workers under stress may start complaining of the warning symptoms of stress, such as headaches, stomach problems, and nausea. Although everyone has bad days physically, managers must be aware of ongoing symptoms.

6. As much as possible and with discretion, **try to understand what may be going on in your subordinates' lives.** For example, one corrections supervisor discovered that one of his staff had a son with a serious medical condition that required frequent medical treatments. The supervisor encouraged the subordinate to keep him informed and if time off was needed, they worked together to ensure that the father was able to take leave for his son. Another subordinate was called into work due to short staffing. While he realized his duty and did not complain, the same supervisor found out that such call-ins created stressful problems because the subordinate had his children certain days of the month due to a divorce settlement.

7. **Encourage the use of stress management tools:** coping techniques, getting in-service training, or using an Employee Assistance Program (EAP), which is discussed later in this chapter.

Improving Working Conditions: Enhancing the Workplace

Correctional supervisors can improve the work environment and decrease stressors that workers encounter. In an organization, any effort at stress management must come from the "top down." Top-level managers and supervisors must make a serious commitment to reduce stress.

Managers must examine what stressors occur in the workplace and make changes. Supervisors also must make themselves highly visible in these actions or employees will be skeptical and pay only "lip service" to suggested changes (Ayres and Flanagan, 1990).

To enhance the workplace, supervisors must be flexible in their thinking and must be willing to try new ideas. Managers and supervisors can use the following guidelines:

1. **Take steps to improve the working environment.** Can offices be less cluttered? Can work items be more practically stored? Can desks or files be rearranged to increase workspace? Can files be restructured to make information more accessible? Can forms be changed to make the job easier?

2. **Encourage upward communication** (Ayres and Flanagan, 1990). Employees like having input into policy and decision making. Supervisors should form employee-advisory committees, include line staff on review committees and task forces, brief staff at roll calls, have suggestion boxes, encourage brainstorming, issue department newsletters, and have "open door" hours. These actions encourage line staff to communicate upward. Suggestions from line staff always should be acknowledged and answered. By doing this, staff will feel they can have a serious impact.

3. **Remain accessible.** Supervisors must not isolate themselves in an office, which discourages informal communication. Supervisors can learn the mood of the office by being receptive to line staff's suggestions or complaints at the same time they demonstrate to their employees that they are interested in what they do. Informal communication forms harmonious, less rigid working relationships between supervisors and line staff. Being accessible means more than just being present in the workplace. It also means (Fulton, 1993):

   - **Being dependable.** Staff should know where you are or how to contact you via radio, pager, phone, cell phone, e-mail, and so forth. It is stressful and frustrating for staff to have to hunt for a supervisor when they need a decision or guidance.

   - **Being friendly and approachable.** By behaving in this way, you will have greater response and success from staff. Keep your office door open as much as possible and encourage staff to stop by with inquiries and ideas. Keep communications open and two-way.

   - **Taking your time.** Time spent with a subordinate is time invested in a stress-reduced workplace. If a subordinate has a problem, treat the individual with high priority.

   - **Building an element of trust.** Take the time, and take an interest in your staff. They will learn to trust you.

4. **Do not assume that because you do not hear any complaints, everyone is happy or the office is running smoothly.** It is wrong to think that just because supervisors do not hear or receive any complaints, grumbling, or criticisms that all is well.

5. **Practice the management by walking around (MBWA) method of supervision** (DeBruyn, 1990). Be mobile. Talk to staff. Spot problems before they get too critical. Get input and form solutions. MBWA builds staff respect.

6. **Be proactive, not reactive.** Do not wait for a problem to get stressful and critical before you react. For example, the jail administrator of a facility plagued by inmate suicides decided after the third suicide in one month to train officers and other staff in suicide prevention. It would have been better to arrange suicide-prevention training immediately after the first suicide, if not earlier. The suicides (and subsequent staff stress) possibly could have been prevented. Playing "catch up" does not work as well as planning ahead.

7. **Rotate work assignments frequently.** Variety in work assignments relieves boredom and allows workers to learn more about the agency. This promotes a positive outlook and prepares workers for promotion.

8. **Promote teamwork.** When workers see themselves as part of a team, the job becomes easier and morale increases because employees are involved with others who feel there is purpose and importance to the work.

9. **Never criticize, put down, or discipline a subordinate in front of others.** One jail officer says:

   "One of the worst supervisors that I ever worked for was a major who would not hesitate to criticize or chastise subordinates in front of the staff. He would call meetings in his office and would interrupt subordinates when they were explaining actions, or turn to other staff and ask them why he should have to put up with a particular staff member (who could not be present) or problem. It got to the point that staff went out of their way to avoid him and when one of his meetings was called, staff would cringe. After such sessions, staff would leave his office frazzled, stressed out, and angry."

10. **Show your appreciation.** You can eliminate the "lack of recognition" stressor by showing appreciation. Everyone in the organization needs recognition—from line staff up through high-level managers. Everyone always can use a sincere pat on the back. Appreciation can be shown in a variety of ways, including the following:

    • Say "thank you" often and sincerely

    • Make a special effort to recognize employee's hard work to solve a problem or finish a project

- Give credit where credit is due by mentioning their names in proposals, reports, or employee newsletters

- Name the workers responsible for outstanding work on projects or departmental activities when briefing other managers or your supervisors

- Write letters of appreciation to workers who perform above average

- Initiate a "Correctional Employee of the Year" program

11. **Acknowledge and reward above-average job performance.** Corrections personnel frequently mention lack of appreciation as a stressor. Most correctional workers realize their pay schedules and raises are dictated by evaluation schedules and other bureaucratic action. However, more than money, most staff believe that recognition by supervisors is the best reward that can be given. Corrections is a profession filled with negatives, such as dealing with offenders who are incarcerated or under supervision against their will, large caseloads, volumes of paperwork, and crowded conditions. Correctional workers need to know that not only are they doing a good job, but that their work is appreciated.

12. **Initiate effective intervention when confronted with a burned-out employee.** Supervisors should take a sincere interest in an employee who is "stressed out." Questions must be clear and to the point. With some workers, the complaints about the stressors may come out in a flood. The supervisor should rank and prioritize these stressors in conjunction with the feelings or emotions of the worker (Reese, 1987). Supervisors should realize that not all stressors can be influenced or changed. Give the employee undivided attention, be patient, control your own emotions, and realize that several conversations may be necessary (Whisenand and Ferguson, 2002). Suggest positive coping techniques, such as time off, exercise, change of diet, and relaxation to burned-out employees. If the symptoms of burnout are in the crisis stage, the supervisor should matter-of-factly tell the employee that professional counseling or help is needed. This may involve asking the employee to go to a mental health counselor about his or her lack of stress management. Ideally, the employee should go voluntarily.

13. **Make basic, self-help recommendations to burned-out employees.** Professional counseling, through a department/agency mental health counselor or employee assistance programs (EAPs) can help tremendously. However, before any effective stress management advice can be given, the supervisor needs to put aside routine concerns and listen to the employee's problem.

Management Styles

Much has been written about how Japanese corporations manage their employees. In the Japanese-management model, supervisors make a significant investment in staff training to enhance worker's performance. Teamwork is promoted, as is individual loyalty to the workplace, by using the philosophy of "command less, persuade more." Supervisors believe that the best motivation is by loyalty and respect. Supervisors and managers in the Japanese model work as part of the team by continuously consulting with subordinates. Workers are valued and the team continuously implements improvements in the workplace.

This is in sharp contrast to the American method of management. In the American method, management and labor (or line staff) are clearly defined and separate. Workers follow instructions while managers do the thinking and planning for the agency. Finally, in many organizations, each worker has a specific job assignment usually with no other responsibilities (Natalucci-Persichetti and Franklin, 1992).

Clearly, there are major differences in the Japanese and American styles. The Japanese style results in the worker having high self-esteem and feeling like an important part of the team. Many correctional agencies in the United States are paramilitary in nature, adhering to rigid controls and rank structure that dictate direction and the way tasks are be performed—from the "top" down. Although many lieutenants, sergeants, and managers in correctional agencies are locked into the rigid system of rank structure and narrowly defined tasks, some elements of the Japanese system, such as consulting with subordinates, can be incorporated. Correctional workers must be encouraged to say, "I think this can work" instead of "it's not my job" when problems and challenges arise.

Are there management styles that cause stress? Yes, there are. These styles have common denominators of not realizing that subordinates want to be treated as valuable people and there is more to life than their view of the job and leadership. These styles cause ill feelings, negative reactions, and stress. If a supervisor wants an unhappy, stressed-out workplace, all he or she has to do is to adapt one of these styles (Whisenand and Ferguson, 2002).

Most likely, all corrections workers at one time or another have encountered the type of supervisor that "makes their skin crawl" and makes a tough job much more difficult. The following types illustrate this point:

Ticket Puncher: This type is a careerist who wants to move up the promotional ladder, and does not let anyone or anything interfere with that. They are hard chargers who thrive on work, work, and more work. Progress is not a high priority. What is important to this worker is being seen as a steady "hard charger" who wants a lot, if not all, of the credit.

Spotlighters: Closely related to the ticket punchers is this group, who craves attention, including media attention, and have to be the center of attention. When things do not go their way, they may quickly disappear and leave others to clean up the mess.

Megadelegators: This type seldom gets his or her desk full of work, or his or her hands dirty. This type delegates much to subordinates and says that he or she is a "participative manager." Eventually the staff realize and resent the fact that they are doing all of the work; the boss is not doing anything.

Micromanagers: The micromanager delegates work, but does not empower the staff to accomplish the task. Subordinates like to learn tasks and strive for accomplishments. However, this type of supervisor constantly is looking over staff's shoulders and checking with them so much on progress, that it drives them crazy. It appears that if this supervisor wants it done his way, he should do it himself. Staff resent not being treated like adults or not being trusted to be allowed to work on something.

One Best Style: These supervisors want you to do a good job, but want you to manage in a way that they think will be successful. There is no way but their way.

I'll Let You Know: These supervisors wander about the workplace or facility and do not say a lot. This is all right until they see something wrong and then they say what is wrong. How is staff supposed to learn what is right or wrong? They cannot read the mind of the supervisor. The supervisor should be taking a continuing interest in what staff is doing. If they are doing it properly, the supervisor should provide praise. This gets the maximum results.

Control Taking: This manager believes in being in charge, being in power, being in control, and being right. They understand the "win-lose" model, not the "win-win." They may say things such as "I am the boss, you are the worker. End of discussion."

Job First: This type gives 110 percent to the job and may be described as a workaholic. They cannot understand that subordinates may not like working long hours or overtime. The job is number one, while the other things in life such as family, hobbies, fun, recreation, and time off are secondary. They feel that the subordinate's first priority in life is the agency. They may go to and support family events, such as banquets, picnics, and so forth. However, they expect staff and their families and friends to participate, too—even if staff's families do not want to go. They are not mean spirited, dictatorial, or manipulative. They do not understand that there is more to life than the job. The job is their main purpose in life and when they retire, the main purpose in their life will be gone.

The Phantom: This is not the same as the job first type. Phantoms are not comfortable around people. They are rarely seen and seldom heard, often using a more personable subordinate to relay orders. The staff encounters three things: infrequent face-to-face conversations, a hurried, semiannual meeting or infrequent staff meetings, and a difficult time getting operational decisions and policy directions. Phantoms are not "people persons."

Employee Assistance Programs (EAPs)

Employee Assistance Programs (EAPs) or stress-assistance programs help employees recognize and overcome stress-related problems that interfere with their work performance. Until the 1980s, the answer to staff members' stress-related problems had been for management to downplay or ignore the problem. With the advancement in knowledge about stress in corrections, some agencies, in cooperation with local community mental-health authorities, have developed EAPs.

EAPs were first developed in the 1980s in response to a growing awareness of substance abuse and its effect on the workplace. EAPs, when properly staffed and used, can help correctional staff effectively deal with their stress. Stress-related programs may include, but are not limited to:

- confidential counseling
- stress-related needs assessment
- physical fitness
- nutritional education and weight control
- spouse training and job familiarization
- stress-management training
- stress-related supervision training
- postcritical event stress/trauma counseling
- peer counseling
- alcohol and drug abuse counseling

(Trautman, 2002)

An EAP or stress program is one of three types (Finn, 2000). An in-house program is a separate unit within the correctional agency that is staffed by trained agency personnel. External programs are private-service providers that contract with the agency to provide services to staff. Hybrid programs use the in-house services of trained personnel and the external services of a contracted provider. There are advantages and disadvantages to each type of program.

With *in-house programs*, staff is likely to be viewed more favorably by personnel seeking help. They feel that the program staff is "one of them." Program staff also is familiar with corrections stress and the department functions. However, there are two disadvantages: correctional workers are more likely to view the program as a tool of upper management and are concerned about confidentiality.

In *external programs*, staff is less likely to view counselors with suspicion, and as a result, they can develop greater trust. Counselors can operate more autonomously and are less likely to be torn between loyalty to the staff and loyalty to the department. Major disadvantages include the program being isolated and workers viewing staff as inaccessible, not part of the corrections community, and as a result, are unfamiliar with corrections' work and stress.

Hybrid programs have many of the advantages of the internal and external programs, with few shortcomings. Hybrid programs combine both outside programs and agency staff who can help with stress management. Procedures should be clear to the employees as to what the outside counselors and the inside counselors can do. For example, an agency can have a contract with a community mental-health center and have officers on hand in the agency trained in stress counseling and peer support. Staff should be aware of what each can do and to whom the officer can be referred. It should be a "we" approach, not a "us or them" approach (Finn, 2000).

An EAP should have the following components to effectively help workers who are suffering from stress and burnout:

1. **Staff knowledgeable about the agency.** EAP counselors should be well versed and familiar with the functions of the agency and the stressors encountered by workers.

2. **Accessible.** The EAP should be accessible to staff at all levels. Referrals can come from supervisors or a procedure for self-referral should be in place.

3. **Support and commitment from management.** Staff should hear from management about how important the EAP is and how it can help. It is counterproductive for staff to see that a sergeant, for example, supports the EAP while his lieutenant thinks that the EAP is a joke.

4. **Confidentiality.** Staff should feel comfortable going to an EAP counselor and know that the problems and treatment discussed are confidential. Staff members should have the opportunity to sign a release-of-information form if it is necessary for other counselors or supervisors to know. The EAP office should be

located away from the agency—where employees may feel their visits will be in confidence.

5. **Referral.** Referrals to EAP usually come from supervisors who have recognized signs of stress in employees. Referrals also should be made for employees who may be suffering from substance abuse, emotional problems, financial problems, and marriage or family problems, because these problems either are stressors or result from stress. The supervisor should follow-up and find out if the employee went to the EAP and is following recommendations and if long-term or short-term treatment is needed.

6. **Networking.** EAP counselors can act as short-term counselors for a few visits. For more serious problems, such as substance abuse and marital problems, the EAP counselor can refer the worker to resources available in the community. EAP staff should have a network of resources for referrals.

EAP Benefits

There are many benefits to having an EAP. EAPs are cost-effective because they offer employers an alternative to firing employees whose personal problems are interfering with their job performance, thus saving the time, money, and staff effort already invested in the employee's future. When an employee with eight, nine, or ten years of experience is fired because of a stress-related problem, not only are wages, benefits, and expenses spent in training gone, but the experience gained is gone, too. This loss of salvageable employees cannot be tolerated in an age of "doing more with less" (Thomas, 1990).

Supervisors should encourage their employees to seek out and use the services of an EAP program. As one corrections supervisor relates:

"I know that using EAP voluntarily is confidential, but I have told my staff that in my career I have used EAP. I do not go into details, but at one time problems at home due to job stress and problem employees were literally driving me up a wall. I went for several months and it was one of the smartest things that I ever did. The alternative was to hold everything in until it would explode. The counselor was very familiar with the prison, and helped me think through some problems that eventually I worked through with my wife. I owe my survival in this field for over twenty-five years to some of the advice that I picked up at EAP."

Since many corrections professionals use EAP and stress programs to deal with crises, EAP programs will be discussed in more detail in Chapter 10.

Stress Management and Direct Supervision

Direct-supervision facilities bring in new considerations in stress management for correctional officers. Unlike other styles of correctional facilities, correctional officers are placed inside the inmate-housing unit, where they must interact with inmates and control them without physical barriers (Allen and Simonsen, 2004). Direct-supervision facilities force staff to communicate with inmates on a personal level never considered by line staff before. Officers cannot stay away from inmates by staying in a hallway or in a control room. Burned-out staff cannot use the flight techniques of avoiding inmates or ignoring them.

Because officers are dealing with inmates directly, they must be even-tempered, level headed, and able to control their stress well. An officer in an inmate dormitory of fifty to sixty inmates cannot "fly off the handle." Not only is this true in direct-supervision facilities, but also in halfway houses and community-corrections centers.

If supervisors in charge of recruiting officers for a new direct-supervision jail housing unit wrote a "wish list" of qualities that they would like in their staff, it would include the following characteristics (McCampbell, 1990):

- interest in maintaining a humane and safe environment
- ability to handle problems with inmates, including discipline and conflicts
- prompt responsiveness to inmate requests
- a clear manner of supervising that indicates organization and the ability to get attention
- ability to build a rapport with inmates and to maintain credibility with them
- ability to get along with other staff

Other qualities would include maturity, professionalism, and a neat appearance. The officer must have a sincere commitment to the concept of direct supervision. There is no room for burnouts.

In a 1991 study by Dr. Linda Zupan at the Santa Clara County Jail in California, correctional staffs working in direct-supervision housing have reported more job satisfaction, lower levels of stress (both overall and on the job), and fewer hassles. The study also indicated that officers in direct supervision might be more satisfied in their jobs (Zupan, Conroy, and Smith, 1991). One of the traditional stressors in corrections has been that workers have little or no control in their jobs. It is clear that direct supervision of offenders gives officers that sense of pride and control that has been lacking in jobs that entail walking the catwalk or sitting in a control booth.

A deputy sheriff lieutenant in Virginia toured several direct-supervision jails in Virginia and Maryland. He was impressed by the staff, which demonstrated a sense of control, pride, and knowledge about their jobs. The most beneficial result is a change of attitude—from one of burnout and negativity to one of satisfaction and pride.

As corrections, especially jails, move forward and progress with new ideas for inmate management, direct supervision is becoming more prevalent. It is becoming clear that staff with good stress-management skills should be staffing these areas.

Learning to Manage Your Time

After reading this chapter, you should understand the following:

- How time can affect the stress you feel

- Why people have problems managing their time

- How to apply time-management techniques to your schedule

- How to organize your life to avoid wasting time

- How to make meetings more effective and less wasteful

Many people report that the lack of time at work and at home is a stressor. Everyone would like an extra hour in the day, or an extra day in the week. It seems that there is not enough time to write the report, shake down the block before lunch, get the chores done, or to just relax. In our fast-paced society, it is not getting any easier. Consider these trends:

- Some national studies have suggested that about sixteen days annually in productivity per worker are lost due to stress, anxiety, and depression (Sharp, 1996).

- Wage earners in the United States log on an extra month of time each year, as compared with workers of the 1970s (Sharp, 1996).

- From 1979-1999, the average work week jumped from 43 to 47 hours (Lardner, 1999).

What does this mean for corrections? It means that shifts can be lacking in staff because stressed out officers call in sick. It means that probation and parole officers are working longer days trying to keep up with paperwork, caseloads, and assignments.

One of the most disconcerting feelings is the pressure of having too much to do in too little time. As corrections moves further into the twenty-first century, job tasks and responsibilities are increasing along with the increasing numbers of offenders. Unfortunately, the number of staff is not. Correctional agencies probably will never have enough people, and a heavy workload will always exist. The problem is how to meet deadlines and meet job responsibilities on time.

All areas of the correctional system have experienced the time crunch. Probation officers in a district office receive word that the circuit-court judges want their presentence reports five days sooner than originally scheduled. Jail-maintenance staff is instructed to expedite repairs on work orders. Classification officers in a jail are ordered to spend less time on intake interviews and more time answering inmate requests, although still maintaining the quality of intake interviews. Clerical staff at a state prison is informed that even though management knows that the workload has doubled, there will be no clerical staff increases for the next budget year. Shift supervisors in a prison are ordered to do quarterly reports for the warden in addition to the monthly and annual reports, and with no additional clerical staff.

Staff members must get their work completed on time, despite limited resources. When workers are 'under the gun,' the pressure of the job magnifies. If an employee is already irritable and angry due to job stress, being faced with more work and time running out can make things worse. For example, Carlos, a jail-booking officer, is on the road to burnout. Over the past several weeks, he has started to act more irritably both at work and at home. One day, with a half-hour to go in his shift, his lieutenant reminds him in a friendly way that a stack of inmate records must be filed by the end of the shift. Carlos starts to sweat and his head begins throbbing. He knows filing the records will take at least an hour to do, and he promised his wife he would not be late. Carlos begins complaining, "I'll get out of this job." He stomps back to the records room, muttering loudly, "Who let these files pile up?"

People do not like to waste time both on and off the job. Because of this, instant foods and microwave ovens were developed, and overnight delivery services do a brisk business. We use e-mail to instantly communicate with people and now do research on the Internet rather than spending hours in a library. Instead of settling down and taking time to read a good book, we now listen to books while driving.

Combined with these other factors is the "information explosion." As reported in the mid 1990s, there were 150,000 books published in the United States, along with 10,000 periodicals, in addition to electronic data that was becoming available (Sharp, 1996). That "information explosion" has now mushroomed into a huge Internet, faster computers, better cell phones, DVDs, more cable television channels, and faster ways

Photo by Gary Cornelius

Just when you think that you have enough to do, your supervisor can bring you a lot more work.

to acquire and read information—in other words—more information to keep up with at work and in our personal lives.

People like to feel they are saving time—both on and off the job. Having too much to do in too little time causes both physical and mental strain. According to David Jenkins, a stress researcher at the University of Texas Medical School, stress caused by poor time management can have serious effects on our health. He says, "Chronic stress, such as that caused by feeling your daily life is out of control, can raise blood pressure and stress hormones, perhaps even lead to heart disease" (Parvin, 1993).

Time management is a constant battle because we all have human frailties, habits, and imperfections. We cannot control all of the interruptions and events (stressors) that life throws at us. With this lack of time come the physical and mental effects of stress: headaches, the panicked rushed feeling, perspiration, irritability, and so on.

The clock cannot be stopped, reversed, or slowed down. Take out your watch or look at a clock. Silently time two minutes. When the two minutes are up, think what you could have done in those two minutes: answered an inmate request? Returned a phone call? Filed three reports? Time is a constant. This fact cannot be changed. What must change is how workers manage themselves in those chunks of time: two minutes or two hours. Time management really means self-management.

Coping with the Time Crunch

A rule to live by is to work smarter, not harder. Quicker does not necessarily mean better. This means applying time-saving techniques in every aspect of life. There are commonsense, simple ways to do this, both on and off the job. What is especially stressful is to spend a busy day on the job and then come home to a lot of demands on precious time. Leisure time, while rare, is important. If workers can manage themselves, they can have more free time for relaxation, positive-coping activities, family time, and doing things to combat burnout. All of these activities counteract the negative effects of stress.

Do you need help with time management? Do you waste time? Is the lack of time affecting the way you live? To find out, take this self-test:

Time Management Self-Assessment

The first step in improving the way we manage time is to do a self-assessment. Look at yourself honestly, and take the following self-test. Please enter your score in the blank space next to each statement. Then, add your scores to compute your total time-management score.

0	1 2 3	4 5 6	7 8 9	10
Never	Sometimes	Frequently	Most of the Time	Always

_____ 1. I am indispensable. I take on tasks because I am the only one who can do them and do them right. My motto is: "If you want something done right, do it yourself."

_____ 2. Daily crises take up all of my time. I seldom work on important things because I am too busy 'putting out fires' and handling problems.

_____ 3. I attempt to do too much at one time, thinking that I can do it all. I infrequently say no.

_____ 4. I feel constant pressure. I feel that I am always behind and cannot catch up. I am always rushing and on the go.

_____ 5. I am working habitually long hours, from ten, and up to eighteen hours per day, five to seven days per week. I never have a day off.

_____ 6. I constantly feel overwhelmed by demands and details. I often do what I do not want to do.

_____ 7. I feel guilty about leaving work on time, as though I did not get every-thing done. I do not have enough time for rest, relaxation, or personal relationships in my life. I take worries and problems from the job home with me.

_____ 8. I frequently miss deadlines, due dates and am late supplying data and information to colleagues.

_____ 9. I am tired and listless, along with many hours of unproductive activity where I get nothing done.

_____ 10. I often go between unpleasant alternatives and am indecisive.

_____ Total Score

Scoring: 35 or less: You could benefit from learning more time-management tech-niques, and your stress level is not significantly impacted by time pressure.

36 to 60: Time-management training would help you and would help in reducing the risk of potential stress disorders and later problems.

Over 60: Your probably often feel that your life is dangerously 'out of control.'

Adapted from: Edward A. Charlesworth, PhD, and Ronald G. Nathan, PhD, 1984.
Stress Management: A Comprehensive Guide to Wellness.
New York, Athenum.

Look at your results. Be honest—is the 'time crunch' making you stressed out?

Time-management experts identify the following four reasons why people have trouble managing their time and getting things done (Walker, 1987):

- failure to set priorities: doing whatever comes their way
- procrastination or putting things off
- doing too much, mostly all at the same time
- trying to do everything perfectly: not delegating or asking for help

About Time

Time is important. It is the way life is measured. Time consultant Alan Lakein says, "Time is life. It is irreversible and irreplaceable. To waste your time is to waste your life" (Lakein, 1973). In corrections, life is tough enough. What you want to strive for is managing yourself efficiently, saving time, and having more time for the positive coping and quality activities that make life good.

Before embarking on a time/self-management improvement program, one should conduct a self-examination, such as the prior test. Ask yourself, "How is my time being wasted?" Time wasters include unexpected visitors, unexpected telephone calls, the inability to find information, cumbersome procedures, unnecessary meetings, vague priorities, and forgetfulness. After identifying how your time is being wasted, you need to be creative about doing what needs to be done. You can invent new and different ways to accomplish more tasks in less time. Brainstorm, and do not hesitate to consider every idea, even if you choose not to try it. You should practice time management every day.

Effective Time or Self-Management

There are effective techniques for time management. The following guidelines are commonsense approaches for managing your time. They can be used at home and at work, whether you are a line officer, juvenile counselor, probation officer, support staff, or supervisor.

Be aware of socializing. Drop-in visitors and social telephone calls are pleasant and stress reducing. But be alert to how time is slipping away. That five-minute gabfest at the coffee pot or on the jail post could run into thirty minutes if you are not careful. The same is true with telephone calls. Before you know it, you have to catch up very quickly and may feel rushed or panicky. Learn to end a conversation with a polite "I have to go," "I'd like to talk, but I must get some work done," or "I'll call you later." At home, if you are busy, there is no harm in telling a caller or visitor that you would like to talk, but you must get back to whatever you were doing. Another possibility for handling telephone calls is leaving the answering machine on and returning social calls when you have time.

Plan your day the day before. One correctional officer lays out his uniform for the next day before he goes to bed, and his wife puts reminders on door jams and mirrors about children's activities, shopping lists, and other household responsibilities. Try a variation of this at work. At the end of the day, lay out the work for the next day.

Get organized and uncluttered. Stress is magnified when we have to look for keys, files, or other items. This is where you must be creative in developing a filing or organizing system that makes things easy to find, especially when you are in a hurry. Organization systems can save you a lot of time—both at work and at home.

Make a to-do list. Time-management experts say this is an excellent way to keep track of things you need to do. Do not depend on memory—write them down and prioritize them. Many time-management experts advocate an A-B-C method of prioritizing: 'A' items are most important, 'B' items are next important or secondary, and 'C' items are least important. Your to-do list should be kept handy. Do not make the mistake of including everyday duties because this could overwhelm you. You also should consider carrying a notepad to write down ideas, information, or tasks as they occur to you (McConkie, 1976).

One supervisor buys bright yellow To Do lists. He writes items in black ink, and checks them off in red, so he can see at a glance how he is doing. He prioritizes items with an asterisk next to his 'A' list. Another correctional supervisor tapes notes to her telephone or desk lamp to make eye-level reminders of important things. *See* the sample in Appendix E.

Make a daily schedule for work and home. Stick to your schedule as best as you can. For example, at home, schedule different chores for different days. At work, schedule blocks of time for tasks. For example, one probation officer allows two hours every morning for file reviews, and an hour before lunch to return calls. In your schedule, allow flexibility for unexpected emergencies, problems, and surprises.

Do not take on too much. Beware of trying to do everything all at once. One correctional officer, who was faced with a lengthy survey, photocopied the lengthy questionnaire, made a worksheet, and divided it into several parts. Instead of doing it all herself, she parceled out sections to other staff who were more familiar with those areas than she was. She gave both the other staff and herself a due date, allowing herself a week before the survey was due to her supervisor. She made a schedule (with flexible time), divided the project into manageable parts, and did not try to do it all herself. At home, if you are faced with a monstrous amount of housework on your day off, do not try to do everything. Divide it up and leave some pleasure time for yourself. Projects and tasks (such as filing) should be divided into parts that can be dealt with easily.

Make unproductive time productive. One correctional officer who teaches a training academy class was behind on his reading. One Saturday, his wife needed him to take her to her office to get some work done. Instead of sitting around for an hour and waiting for her in the car, he took his reading with him and finished it. Waiting in a long line also can be productive. While waiting, you can read or make up a grocery list (Walker, 1987). Use time in front of the television to exercise or sort clothes. Small bits of time also can be useful. One probation officer had a ten-minute wait before leaving for lunch with a colleague. In that ten minutes, the probation officer returned telephone calls and filed several reports, instead of just sitting and waiting. Five-, ten-, or fifteen-minute periods should not be wasted. This is especially true when waiting for court: take something that you have been meaning to read.

Schedule like activities together. If telephone messages have piled up, line them up and return them all at once. If you have a lot of appointments, try to schedule them during blocks of time, such as 8 to 11 a.m. and 1 to 3:00 p.m. If you like getting off work on time, avoid scheduling appointments close to quitting time whenever possible.

Combine tasks. Going upstairs at home? Can anything go up with you? Or when going to check your mailbox at work, see if you need to photocopy anything on the same trip. You always should be on the lookout for tasks that can be combined.

Do not procrastinate. All correctional workers encounter people and tasks that they find distasteful. A jail officer may get to her post and learn that a particular inmate wants to see her. The officer knows this inmate is difficult to talk to and is very manipulative. The officer has the time and a choice—to see this inmate now or later. The best choice is to see the inmate now and get it out of the way before her day fills up with other problems and tasks. A probation officer with a lengthy presentence report to write should do it first and get it out of the way. Whenever possible, do the hardest, most difficult tasks first. By doing so, difficult tasks that are put off will not 'surprise' you at the end of your day. This means seeing disagreeable inmates or counseling a staff member. No one *likes* to do these tasks, but wouldn't you rather do them at the beginning of your day or shift?

Look ahead and keep the end result in mind. If you are involved in an ongoing project, employ procedures that will get the results you want without backtracking. For example, Mike, a work-release supervisor, had to submit a yearly report to his sheriff concerning characteristics, such as level of education, drug usage, age, and charge, of offenders enrolled in the program. Offenders' demographic information was logged in a branch log. Offenders' names and charges were logged in a division master log. At the end of the year, Mike discovered that the division master log was not accurate. With the report due in a few weeks, Mike had to spend precious time going back through two logs to correct mistakes. If Mike had checked periodically to verify that data were entered correctly, he could have avoided the extra work.

The same principle can be applied to ordering supplies—do not wait until you are completely out of office supplies to reorder.

Delegate clearly. Delegating at home or at work can save time. Make sure you clearly state the task and your expectations and give your employees all the information they need to know. Trust your 'gut.' If you think the other person may not understand the instructions, ask for feedback. Put instructions in writing, if necessary.

Hold effective meetings. A sure "downer" is to hold meetings that staff members consider a waste of their time. Staff members may feel that nothing—or very little—gets done and their time could be put to better use. Not everyone likes going to meetings or thinks meetings are productive. Meetings should facilitate communication and promote teamwork. However, ask yourself frequently: is this meeting really necessary, or can the issues be handled in a conversation, phone call, or by e-mail? Do all staff have to attend or should I allow only the critical staff to attend?

Making Meetings More Effective

The following guidelines can make meetings more productive, build morale, and save time:

- schedule meetings as early in the day as possible—not late in the day when workers are trying to "wrap up" or are handling problems
- choose a place that has comfortable seating and allows for note taking
- distribute a written agenda in advance to allow participants to prepare
- limit socializing (which is okay before the meeting, but not after the meeting starts)
- start promptly on time, and end on time. Take breaks, but limit their length
- designate a recorder of minutes and then distribute minutes within one or two workdays
- stick to the agenda by being businesslike and announcing each item
- watch the time and limit discussions of topics to a reasonable amount of time
- make decisions or delegate assignments
- limit interruptions (although everyone should have a chance to speak, comments should be brief). Put on the phone answering machine
- end on time and remember that workers have jobs to get back to
- do not circle! Move on to the next topic. Try not to 'back track' and revisit ground that you already have walked through

Triumphing over Disorganization

Here are some tried and true methods for organizing those daily duties that can waste so much of your time. Try the following suggestions:

- keep a wastebasket handy to throw things away immediately. Do not read junk mail. Throw it away. Keep only one copy of a document

- label shelves, drawers, binders, and files clearly

- keep your keys on a key rack and your essentials (wallet, purse, ID, badge, and so forth) in a designated place

- designate a "drop off point" in the house for lunches, mail to be sorted, and so forth

- put things away as soon as you use them, wear them, or read them

- have a laundry hamper or bins to presort wash, and set a deadline (Friday at 10 p.m., for example) so family members have their wash in one place and ready to go

- assign chores to everyone (both at home and at work), so that everyone has a specific job and knows what it is

- write down dates of events on one calendar. Use a color system to designate priorities

- keep a rolodex, telephone book, or personal digital assistant (pda) updated at home and at work or use the computer to keep numbers and addresses

- purge or clean out files, drawers, closets, briefcases, and purses on a regular basis—every week, every other month, or annually

- file papers every day, if possible. If you cannot file right away, at least write in a corner of the document into what file it goes.

- make a file for household warranties, appliance instructions, and information on items purchased for home improvements in case replacements are needed

- have your desk calendar and to-do list easily visible and not covered up on your desk

- have a clean workspace

- try not to use scraps of paper or "sticky notes." They can get lost. Try to work from one calendar or list.

- plan ahead: make lunches in advance. Make several meals and freeze them.

An hour is a lot of time. Often we think—If I only had an hour to myself, or just one hour a day to do what I want to do. Noted authors Steven Covey and Hyrum Smith say that the following tips may be able to save you one hour per day (Covey and Smith, 1999):

- Banish interruptions, such as the workplace social star or the chatterbox neighbor, who cut into productive work time or task/chore time. Politely say "no" or beg off. According to Covey, a recent business study found that people spend almost four hours per week handling interruptions. If one half of those are reasonable and valid interruptions, that means two hours per week are chitchat. Spread the time saved over seven weekdays: **Time saved per day: 17 minutes**

- Delegate the laundry to someone else, saving an average of fifty-four minutes per week per load: **Time saved per day: 8 minutes**

- Prepare for meetings: The length of some meetings could be cut in half if workers were prepared. One survey, Covey states, found that people reported spending 2.1 hours per week in meetings for which they had not prepared. **Time saved per day: 9 minutes**

- Pay someone to do your yard work: Over the year, people spend an average of three hours in the fall working in their yards. If someone did it for you, such as a neighborhood teenager who needs the money, you could save twenty-five minutes a day in the fall, or spread it out over a year. **Time saved per day: 6 minutes**

- Use a cell phone when standing in a line, and so forth. Make the necessary calls or schedule appointments. **Time saved per day: 3 minutes**

- Plan dinner menus in advance over the coming week, buying all of the necessary food in advance: **Time saved per day: 6 minutes**

- Batch tasks together: read mail in one batch, return calls in one batch, make a birthday list by month, buy the cards altogether in one batch, and so forth: **Time saved per day: 2.5 minutes**

- Pay bills electronically. This can save one hour and forty-five minutes per month. **Time saved per day: 3.5 minutes**

- Get up earlier. Read, do a chore, and so forth before you start your workday. **Time saved per day: 5 minutes**

TOTAL TIME SAVED PER DAY: 1 hour

What are some corrections professionals doing? Here are some tips from several correctional counselors and probation and parole officers:

- Learn to say "no" without feeling guilty.

- Make a running list of tasks and cross-out accomplishments. Even if you think that you have not accomplished anything, look at your list and you will see that you have. Mark tasks in order of importance. Know that you may not do be able to do them all in one day. Keep your list handy. Jot down a goal for the day.

- Take a laptop computer into the field. Log information in breaks between home/job visits. Use it during lunch if you are in a quiet place.

- If you have to make a phone call, pick a time when you are most likely to get the person's machine. By doing so, you will not be drawn into social, nonproductive conversations.

- Set aside days or allotments of time for paperwork only. On paperwork days, do not set appointments. Vary your schedule to escape the phones: come in early or stay late. Start with priority paperwork such as violations or presentence reports, and end with filing.

- Know yourself: Do the hardest and most disliked tasks first!

- Make your TO DO list for the next day the day before during a quiet time and in a quiet place. Do not do it in the morning because you will be interrupted.

- Use dead time: while waiting in court for a case to be called, in a doctor's office, and so forth. Take material to read, write or rewrite, or proof. Use your cell phone and get some calls out of the way.

- If not in the mood for something difficult, do the rote things, such as filling in parts of forms that are routine and do the more complicated parts later, when you are up to it and in a quiet place and time.

- Think ahead. When seeing clients in the community or at a correctional facility, try to get the little chores done: get gas for the car, pick up the dry cleaning, and so forth.

- Learn gradually to be "multitask oriented." Start off with one task at a time, and as you develop your skills and self-management techniques, learn how to work on several things at once.

- Do a self-exam. Take a hard, but realistic look at yourself. What are you doing that wastes time? Are you the office/facility social gadfly, the clown, or the gossip champion?

- Do you always need to be included in every social gathering or conversation? Are you easily distracted? If you answer "yes," then ask: why? Try to understand these faults and try to improve yourself.

Time management means self-management. Frequently ask yourself—what can I do right now, in this space of five minutes, ten minutes, or twenty minutes? Self-management must be practiced. The stress you save will be your own.

Learning to Relax:
On and Off the Job

After reading this chapter, you should understand the following:

• Why relaxing is not a waste of time

• The physical and mental benefits of relaxation

• How to use relaxation techniques at home and at work

Perhaps the most important positive coping technique that correctional workers should learn is how to relax. If you can relax, you can go a long way in managing your stress. Relaxation can recharge a drained correctional worker's batteries. The supply of adaptive energy is renewed after the body and mind have had a chance to take a break and rest. Relaxation is the ultimate in doing something nice for yourself, and it costs next to nothing. All that is required is a desire to counteract the negative effects of stress with time and imagination.

Physical and Mental Benefits

To fully appreciate the benefits of relaxation, you should understand its physical and mental benefits. Throughout a relaxation activity, you should concentrate on how you feel.

Physical Effects

Relaxation calms the body down. In the alarm-and-adaptation stages of stress, the body is keyed up, tensed, and ready to meet the threat or flee. As we have seen, heart beat increases, muscles are tight, heavy perspiration begins, and the body undergoes numerous changes. If these conditions continue as our stress reaction continues, it takes a toll on our bodies and behavior. Relaxation methods can counteract these physical and behavioral responses. One way to tell is through biofeedback, where these responses and changes due to relaxation are monitored by sophisticated equipment. But there are simple ways that you can monitor yourself without equipment (Powell, 1992). These methods include the following:

1. Check your pulse before and after relaxation. If you are relaxed, your pulse will be lower.

2. Check your perspiration. One officer said that when he is under stress, his brow becomes wet with perspiration, and he can feel sweat running down his back.

3. Check your hand temperature. A hand-held thermometer can be used to see if you are relaxing. The warmer your hand is, the more relaxed you are (Powell, 1992).

4. Feel your muscles. Are they tense? Is your neck or back sore?

5. Are you acting tense? Are you drumming your fingers or grinding your teeth? Many of us do these things without realizing it. Are you snappy or irritable?

6. Do you have a headache? If you do, you probably are tense.

7. Do a "mirror" test. Look at yourself in a mirror. Do you look tired? Are your eyes bloodshot, watery, red, or puffy? Does the way you look tell you "I need to relax" (Powell, 1992)?

Checking for the physical and mental signs of tension is simply getting in touch with how you are feeling overall. You should check yourself out before and after relaxing. The differences will be clear.

Mental Benefits

Mentally, relaxation can help us get rid of the tensions caused by stressors. Relaxation allows our minds to wander from the bothers, concerns, and worries that are part of our everyday life. It recharges our mental faculties. It also helps us to focus away from the negative and see and appreciate the positive things in our lives. These positive things are sometimes people—our friends, families, and significant others who we do not want to snap at, hurt, or alienate. If dad is relaxed after a long difficult shift at the prison, he will participate in a family activity. If a probation/parole officer relaxes after a difficult visit with a client, she will rebound with extra energy to get some more work done.

Without relaxation, we will stay keyed up and tense, which will only hurt us in the long haul. When combined with poor health habits, such as smoking, overeating, and not exercising, we are a heart attack waiting to happen.

Skeptical? Consider the results of a study of 192 British men and women, ages thirty-five to sixty-four, who were at risk for heart disease due to hypertension, smoking, and high levels of cholesterol. These men and women were divided into two groups. Researchers gave both groups instructions on how to change their bad habits, such as quitting smoking and lowering their blood pressure. However, one group received instructions, one hour per week, on stress management, including being taught exercises on breathing and meditating (both of which are relaxation techniques). The results were significant. Eight months later, the group trained in relaxation techniques had lower blood pressure and smoked fewer cigarettes than the group that did not have the stress-management training. Four years later, the stress-management group had a lower rate of hypertension and heart disease (Benson et al., 1987).

In private industry, just as in public service, workers want relief from stress. Stress-management experts also recommend relaxation methods, such as abdominal breathing, meditating, imaging (thinking of mental scenes or pictures that create warm feelings), and "perceptual restructuring." Allen Elkin, program director of Stresscare, a stress management consulting firm, recommends the latter method, which is simply not worrying about the little things. Elkin also says that people "have a tendency toward 'catastrophizing' and 'awfulizing'" (Miller et al., 1988).

It is true that correctional workers sometimes worry about things over which we have no control or that really are not crucial. We see people "sweating the small stuff" all the time, such as a probation officer worrying that she will not be able to return all her telephone calls, a jail clerk trying to finish filing a stack of noncritical material in one day and agonizing over it, and a supervisor "flipping out" about a cancelled meeting. We sometimes worry too much.

Relaxing is not being lazy or unproductive. To the uninformed, a person lying on a couch with his or her eyes closed may appear to be lazy. But someone in the know will understand that the person may be relaxing after a particularly stressful day. For example, a parole district supervisor notices Jack, a parole officer, getting up from his desk and walking outside during a busy day. The supervisor may think that Jack is being inattentive and wasting time, but if the supervisor understands stress management, he probably will realize that Jack is taking a much-needed break.

Relaxation techniques can be varied in method and length of time. A worker can devote as much as thirty minutes a day to relax or as little as five minutes a day. Whatever method is used and for how long depends on the environment and the circumstances under which we want to relax. For instance, if a juvenile counselor encounters many stressful situations throughout a busy workday, he or she probably will not have a thirty-minute block of time to relax, and a prison officer cannot just get up and leave his or her post for a quiet break. At home, faced with children, bills to

Photo by Joseph J. Fuller, ACA.

Taking a break—"chilling out" or just telephoning a friend or loved one can ease the burdens of a stressful workday and take the "edge off."

pay, or household chores, many workers find it hard to relax for an hour. It is important to remember that there are methods that do not take a lot of time. Remember, too, that the idea of relaxation, no matter what the technique, is to turn off the alarm in our bodies and to calm down.

Triggers of Relaxation

Cheek developed relaxation techniques that we can use when our bodies signal we are under stress and need to calm down. These techniques can be "at our command" and can quickly switch off tension in situations on and off the job (Cheek, 1984). These methods include the calm scene, countdown-count up, code words, and deep breathing. (*See* Appendix D for more detailed explanations and instructions for these techniques).

Calm Scene

Using the calm-scene method simply means taking a moment to think of a place or image you like that makes you feel warm and relaxed. It could be a place where you vacationed, a particular room in your home, or a place in your backyard. It can be used anytime. For example, Diane, a classification officer at a county jail, and her partner have conducted twenty intake interviews on newly arriving inmates. An hour before the end of the shift, it looks as if they will get off on time for a change. Then, a call comes in from the booking desk. A raid by local police has netted sixteen new arrests. The jail administrator wants them interviewed and moved out of receiving that night. This means more work and overtime for Diane on a day when she was looking forward to going home on time. She is under stress. She has begun to perspire heavily and she feels a headache coming on. What she needs to do is calm down, relax, and get the job done. She tells her partner that she is going to take a five-minute break; then, she sits comfortably at her desk and takes a few deep breaths. She closes her eyes and, still breathing deeply, thinks of the beach house where she vacationed last summer. She can see the sun going down, hear the waves, and she almost feels the sea breeze. After thinking about the beach scene for a few minutes, Diane opens her eyes slowly, takes another deep breath, and notices that she feels better. Now, she is ready to tackle this stressor with charged-up energy instead of nervous fatigue.

Using Visual Imagery

Imaging is similar to the calm scene. It involves focusing your mind on pleasant thoughts and images and creating a picture in your mind. Imaging can reduce stress and lower high blood pressure. All you have to do is sit comfortably, close your eyes, breathe deeply, and think of an image that is relaxing to you: a meadow, a sunrise over the ocean, your backyard, a favorite song, an event from your life, or a favorite pet. You should do this for five, ten, or twenty minutes.

Imaging can be used for a "dress rehearsal" for events that put you under stress. Salespeople, athletes, actors, and performers often use this technique. Rehearsing means to imagine yourself being calm, relaxed, and confident in a situation that puts you under stress. Thus, when the real situation occurs, you will feel calm and relaxed (Powell, 1992).

For example, Ann, a lieutenant at a state prison, is going before a promotion board to qualify for captain in three days. She has studied, but is tense and anxious. She needs to relax. She recently went through stress-management training offered by her facility, so she recognizes that she is under stress and knows some simple techniques to try to reduce it. To reduce her stress, she goes through the following simple steps:

1. Sitting comfortably, she closes her eyes, breathes deeply and unwinds, concentrating on this relaxing sensation.

2. She imagines herself actually before the promotion board, feeling calm.

3. She visualizes the scene over and over, putting in as many details as she can: her appearance, the room, the questions.

4. She imagines a positive outcome, with her answering questions correctly.

By the time Ann goes to the promotion board, she will feel relaxed and ready.

Countdown

This method involves simply counting down from ten to one or counting up from one to ten while breathing deeply when faced with a stressor. For example, Ray, a probation officer, has been working on a pre-sentence report. He feels tense and knows he is under pressure to meet the court's deadline. The telephone rings and the receptionist says that the offender's attorney wants to see him. Ray knows that this particular attorney will argue tooth and nail for her client. It is an interruption that Ray does not need. Ray leans back in his chair, takes three deep breaths, and slowly counts down from ten to one. While he counts, he breathes in and out slowly from his abdomen. He is now relaxed, less tense, and ready to meet the attorney.

Code Words

Some workers use code words along with deep breathing to relax. The code word tells you to relax and calm down. Your code word can be whatever you want. For example, Beverly, a work- release supervisor, would breathe deeply and say, "Oh well" when she faced a problem or a crisis. The phrase "oh well" did not mean the problem was not important, but that although she could not control all stressors, she could handle this one. Other code words or phrases could be "calm down," "take it easy," "relax," "slow down," or "I can handle this."

Deep Breathing

If you feel a little self-conscious using code words or counting, even though saying code words or counting can be done silently, practice deep breathing, which will also help you relax. Deep breathing exercises can be varied. Dr. Jenny Steinmetz, a psychologist for Kaiser Permanente, says that "taking four deep breaths with a seven-second inhale and an eight-second exhale is the quickest way to reverse the effects of stress" (Meade, 1992). As we breathe out slowly, much of the built-up tension is expelled outward. Deep breathing can be performed anytime and anywhere—between intake interviews in a jail, after a difficult appointment with a parolee, after breaking up a fight between two juveniles, or during a lull in the activity at the booking desk.

The Wonders of Imagination

Some stress researchers report that stressed-out people use a variety of imaginative images to relax. How about a ten to fifteen minute "burlap sack" exercise (Pfeiffer and Webster, 1992)?

In a quiet place:
Close your eyes.
Breathe normally.
Imagine yourself as a burlap bag full of sand, full of pent-up tension.
The bottom corners of the bag are your feet.
The corners suddenly burst open and the sand starts to run out.
Feel the sand run out of your feet, and all the tension you feel running out, too.
Completely empty the bag of all of the sand and all of the tension.
Resume your normal activity.

Others use the "color" method (Powell, 1992). Sit relaxed and imagine two colors—one such as red that represents tension, and pale blue, which means relaxation. With your eyes closed, imagine that your muscles are the tense color. Imagine each muscle changing to the relaxed color from red to blue over your whole body. Now, think of your body as a whole hue of the relaxed color. You see yourself as entirely relaxed.

Another method is to use the "painting a picture" technique (Powell, 1992). Instead of abstract things such as colors, try imagining tension as tangible things such as rocks on a beach. Then, imagine a picture of relaxing things like ocean waves steadily washing over the rocks, smoothing out the rocks' surface.

Practicing Progressive Relaxation

First called "Progressive Deep Muscle Relaxation" by Dr. Edmund Jacobson, who invented it, this technique is now referred to as *progressive relaxation*. When done properly, progressive relaxation can release built-up tension and stress and leave you feeling relaxed for hours. Research has shown progressive relaxation can reduce the severity of stress ailments, such as hypertension, headaches (including migraines) due to tension, anxiety, insomnia, and muscle tension (Benson et al., 1987).

To practice progressive relaxation, you systematically tense and relax each muscle group in your body, from head to toe. While doing so, you should breathe deeply. You can perform the exercise by silently telling yourself what to do or by listening to a voice on an audio cassette tape. *See* Appendix D for an example of a progressive-relaxation exercise.

Stretching to Relax

Stretching exercises help us feel relaxed. As you feel yourself tensing up, stretch for a few minutes. Stretching can be done in the morning upon awakening, after getting out of a cramped vehicle after a ride to or from work, at your desk, or during a pause in your cellblock rounds. Stretching exercises may include the following:

- rotating your head and neck from side to side slowly—three to five times
- closing your eyes, opening your mouth, and dropping your jaw as much as possible
- putting your arms straight out in front of you and stretching them, as though you are pushing an imaginary object
- doing ten arm circles by putting your arms straight out at your sides with your fingers pointed up and rotating your arms in circular motions

Establishing Tranquil Environments

Some relaxation techniques can be used quickly in a work environment, such as deep breathing, code words, the countdown-count-up, and stretching. Other techniques can be used in offices or at home in more relaxed environments.

The surroundings we relax in should be tranquil or soothing. Soothing environments can be established for our bodies and minds by hanging pictures on the walls, having the office decorated with pleasant, personal mementos, and listening to soothing music (Witkin-Lanoil, 1986). One probation officer has an aquarium in her office. She likes watching her fish because they keep her calm. A community corrections supervisor enjoyed displaying school paintings from his daughter. Another had several magazines or a favorite book in his desk drawer. During the day he would pause for a few minutes and read something that has nothing to do with work, but gives his mind a mental break.

Let your home be your "stress refuge." After a long day of dealing with inmates, supervisors, and other stressors, a worker should be able to relax in pleasant surroundings—a home that is pleasing to the eye and as uncluttered as possible. Music can be important at home, too. If you feel tense, think: "I'm home." Sit quietly to relax, and put on your favorite music. One deputy, before going to sleep at night, listens to his favorite music through headphones—it relaxes him.

Soaking in a warm bath, taking a shower, or floating in a pool can create a feeling of tranquility that blends well with an imaging or progressive-relaxation exercise. One juvenile counselor draws a hot bubble bath, puts on some soft music, leans back in the tub, closes her eyes, and imagines she is walking through a sunlit meadow. A prison officer comes home, kicks off his shoes, relaxes on a reclining easy chair in silence, and practices progressive relaxation. A jail officer told the author that he likes to come home and sit on his back patio with a cold drink, and watch his dog play in the yard. No matter how bad his day is, he says, he knows that he can do that when he gets home and the house is quiet.

Do not let your calm, tranquil environment be disrupted by children knocking on the door or the telephone ringing. Remember, you control the environment. Let the answering machine get the telephone and ask the children not to interrupt you unless there is an emergency. Relaxation time is yours.

More Relaxers

There are many ways to relax—more than this book can cover. Each person has individual ways he or she relaxes, and people try new ways to relax throughout their lives. Do not be afraid to experiment to discover which relaxation methods work best for you. Some people practice a variety of relaxation methods or alternate methods to meet their different needs. Performing minimeditations, napping, watching videos, listening to music, listening to subliminal tapes, and engaging in spiritual practices all can help you relax.

Using Minimeditations

Dr. Jon Kabat Zinn, director of the Stress Reduction Clinic at the University of Massachusetts Medical Center, says that while under stress, our minds are "stormy and agitated." Several times a day, with durations from a few seconds to a few minutes, allow yourself to be aware of what is around you—a fragrance, a breeze, flowers, and so forth. Watch people, cars, the sky, a bird flying past your office window. Eat slowly, savor the flavor of food, feel the cool drink as it slides down your throat. Your tension will be relieved and your mind will be reenergized (Perlmutter, 1991).

Napping

Some people take naps to relax. Although this is impractical at work, you could lie down for thirty minutes or an hour when you get home. Taking a nap relaxes you and recharges the energy you need to deal with stress (Evans, 1993).

Watching Videos

We now live in the age of video: videocassettes and DVDs. Just about everything we like to see is on video and DVD, including relaxing scenes. If you enjoy watching movies or television shows you have taped, set aside some time, pop some popcorn, stretch out, and watch a movie.

Using "Sound" or Music Relaxation

Some of us like soothing sounds, from rippling brooks to soft rain on a rooftop. Other examples include the sounds of birds, wind chimes (which you can buy and hang near an open window), or the surf pounding on the beach. Put a tape on, close your eyes, and imagine a calm scene. One couple goes to sleep every night with a tape of soft rain playing. Many of these sounds are on cassette tapes or compact disks sold in music stores.

The right kind of music is one of the best stress reducers. Listening to the music you like gives you a pleasant lift, but if you are tense and your mind is racing due to a stressful day, "New Age" music is probably the best to help you relax. New Age music is usually instrumental, soft, and pleasant. Meant for relaxation, it helps your mind wander. Researchers say that the best way to enjoy New Age music is to be comfortable and "float" along with the music for at least fifteen minutes. This type of music can be played anywhere: in the office, in the car, or around the house. And why get up in the morning with a jolt? Have this type of music or easy listening music tuned into your radio alarm, not rock and roll. Relaxing music can let you awaken feeling rested. You always can switch stations as you are getting dressed to get fired up.

Listening to Subliminal Tapes

Subliminal tapes feature relaxing music or sounds of the environment, together with stress-reducing messages that cannot be consciously heard. Advocates of subliminal relaxation say that these messages, directed at our unconscious minds, help us to reduce tension and stress.

Engaging in Spiritual Relaxation

Praying and spiritual meditation may be a good way to relax. Finding a quiet time and place to think, reflect, and meditate to a higher being depending on one's beliefs, can serve to calm and reduce tension. According to one study, reciting rhythmic formulas, rites, or prayers such as the Ave Maria combined with yoga exercises has a marked, measurable effect on the cardiovascular system (Maltin, 2001). No matter what your beliefs are, pausing, deep breathing, and praying or seeking guidance can help you calm down.

One final note: in a correctional setting it is hard to get to a quiet place and relax. However, work something out with your supervisor and colleagues. If you feel the need to calm down before you "go off" on an inmate or officer, ask for a break from your post. This is especially true after you have handled a serious incident.

Making Your Life Plan

After reading this chapter, you should understand the following:

- How to develop a personalized plan for stress reduction

- How to develop and maintain both physical and mental wellness

- Why family support is so important to stress management

Now that you know about stress, stressors, and positive-coping techniques, you can begin to make changes in your life. Why is change so important? By making changes, you are more likely to live a healthy, long, and fulfilling life. Changing negative coping habits will help you live up to your full potential and enrich the quality not only of your everyday life, but the lives of those around you—your family and loved ones. Developing a personalized plan for change can be compared to fighting a battle when positive-coping habits must win over negative ones to achieve the objective—a good life. Developing a plan must focus on two levels—physical and mental—using the concept of wellness.

Wellness

Wellness in corrections means "health promotion and the prevention of psychological and physiological problems in correctional workers" (Verdeyen, 1992). Another way to look at it is to live a lifestyle in which your actions promote being as healthy as possible. Workers who believe in wellness practice this everyday. They eat nutritious foods, get enough rest, exercise, watch their weight, have hobbies, avoid abusing drugs and alcohol, do not smoke, and practice relaxation. They also learn to talk to others, seek help when they are stressed out, and do not hold stress in.

Humor and good friendly relationships with others are positive-coping mechanisms.

Your strategy for stress management should include the philosophy of wellness. It takes commitment. Change is not easy, especially if you are not used to regularly exercising, enjoy junk food, or smoke. Bad habits such as these cannot be changed immediately. If you have not worked out since your rookie days at the academy, you cannot just get up tomorrow and run five miles. Your system cannot take the shock. You will get sore, winded, and discouraged. Change not only must be determined, but gradual.

Some workers can make the changes over a few weeks time; some may take several months or even a year. The important thing is to get started. Improved creativity, thinking, decisiveness, motivation, positive attitude, high morale, and improved interpersonal skills are just some of the benefits of wellness through stress management. Increased stamina and energy, better muscular strength and flexibility, an overall feeling of good health, resistance to disease, and improved appearance are a few physical benefits. Developing a strategy is a big step and requires planning. Occasionally, you might skip exercises or eat junk food—nobody is perfect. But remember, when you go "off the track," you can get back on.

For example, Linda, a probation officer, usually eats a healthy lunch of salad or fruit. But on Thursday—her day to conduct field visits—she forgot to pack her lunch. At lunchtime, she finds herself rushed and grabs a big hamburger and a milkshake. Linda slipped, but vows to eat a healthy dinner and take a brisk walk that evening to burn off the extra calories. Her mindset is wellness. The long-term result is stress management.

A common mistake is to try to make too many changes too fast. The other "players" involved—coworkers, spouse, loved ones, and children—need to be informed of your plans. If you try to take on too many changes, you may find yourself succeeding at some, but not at others. This can be discouraging. Plan to make gradual changes.

Setting Goals

You should have short-term and long-term goals in mind when designing your plan. You must look ahead and decide where you want your stress-management techniques to take you. Long-term goals must be kept in focus when making your plan because the long-term goal is the end result. Short-term goals help you get there. Goals must meet five basic criteria. They must be specific; measurable; agreed to by you and others, such as your spouse and children, involved in your stress-management plan; reachable; and timed. Together they spell SMART (Cornelius, 1991).

Be specific. Instead of saying, "I want to improve my health," identify a specific goal, such as swimming laps and working up to one mile a week, walking one mile every day, relaxing for thirty minutes after work, and listening to music at work. Instead of saying "I have to relax," identify what you actually can do, such as taking a nap after work before the family comes home, going on a leisurely walk, and so forth.

Be measurable. Pick activities and goals that can be measured—walking one mile per day, doing a step-aerobic activity every other day, or losing five pounds per month with a proper diet plan and exercise.

Be agreed to. You and those important in your life must agree to your goal. Quitting smoking is a good example. If you have smoked three packs a day for twenty years and decide you want to quit, you should tell your spouse of your goal—to quit smoking—and ask for his or her support. You should mention that it will be rough because of mood changes and cravings for cigarettes. Your spouse should agree this is important to you and be supportive. If your spouse smokes, it might be a good time to quit together. Both of you should accept the importance of your goals. You also should support your spouse's goals. Another aspect to this is eating habits. For example, if you have been a big eater for most of your life, you may have to make significant changes in your home environment concerning bringing home fatty foods or junk foods. Others in your home may like these foods, and you all may have to agree to some rules about how much there is, and so forth

Be reachable. Goals should not be unrealistic. If you want to lose twenty pounds, do not set a goal of losing twenty pounds in two weeks—set a timetable of six months. If you are starting to jog, do not expect to run five miles the first week. Take your time and remember that you are making a *long-term investment.*

Be timed. When you plan your goals, use dates. If today is January 1, decide that by June 1 you want to be twenty pounds lighter. If you cannot quit smoking quickly, make your goal to be down to one pack a day within thirty days.

For example, if your long-term goal is to improve physical health, then make your short-term goals to lose ten pounds in sixty days, start a low-fat diet, and start walking a mile a day on a specific date. If your long-term goal is to make relaxation a normal part of your life, then make your short-term goals to practice deep breathing daily in short breaks at work and to practice relaxation by listening to soft music in bed before going to sleep.

By keeping long-term goals in mind, it makes it easier for you to plan your strategy. Short-term goals are the building blocks to meeting the long-term goal. One jail deputy made his long-term goal to improve his cardiovascular system. He subsequently met the following short-term goals: within three years he had quit using all tobacco products (he smoked cigarettes, cigars, and a pipe), he began walking a mile several times a week, and during the summer he swam laps.

Charting Your Goals

Like any plan, it is advisable to write down your long-term and short-term goals. Devising a personalized stress-management plan should be a well-thought-out process. Start charting your goals by listing your long-term goals and any obstacles to them. Then, list your short-term goals and strategies to overcome the obstacles.

For example, Tony, a parole officer, looks around his office and realizes it is extremely cluttered with files, unanswered correspondence, and miscellaneous paperwork. His desk is buried beneath papers. His Rolodex needs updating, his e-mail files need to be deleted, and his desk drawers are full. The clutter is creating a lot of stress because he cannot find files or telephone numbers. He makes his long-term goal to get his office organized. The obstacles in the way are a heavy schedule, client appointments, staff meetings, field visit days, and court appearances. Then, Tony decides that the most helpful short-term goals should be to clean out desk drawers in the first week, prioritize correspondence to read in the second week, purge inactive files in the third week, and reorganize his filing system in the fourth week. Tony's strategies will focus on practicing time management. He will try to schedule appointments far enough apart to leave time to work on his goals in between. He also will break down the tasks involved for each short-term goal: if pressed, he will do one drawer a day and will try not to worry about completing his short-term goals on field visit or court days.

Rhonda, a jail officer, is stressed out because her home is cluttered and this is getting on her nerves. It seems that she and her husband are always cleaning or looking for things. They cannot relax. She establishes a long-term goal of making their home a "stress refuge." The obstacles to the goal are her shift work combined with her husband's work schedule, two teenage children, many outside activities, and different opinions about who should be responsible for certain household chores. Rhonda's short-term goals are to get chores organized within one week, to get a cleaning schedule operating within two weeks, and to communicate to her family the importance of keeping the house clean as soon as possible. Her strategies are to have a family meeting to discuss how clutter is causing stress and what each can do to help; to work out a mutually agreeable schedule around work schedules, school, and family activities; and to organize chores on a month's trial basis.

Not every long-term goal will have obstacles, but by thinking about them at the beginning, you prepare yourself for pitfalls along the way. You do not want to be taken by surprise. You can chart your plan in any number of ways, from simply jotting your strategies down on a notepad and keeping it visible to using a form you can devise yourself. It is important to keep in mind what the stressors are doing to you. Are they affecting you mentally and/or physically? In Appendix E, there is an example of a personalized plan form. Use it or devise one that works for you. Some people keep a diary so they can record their progress (or lack of it) and how they are feeling. Writing your observations can be beneficial. By writing your feelings and documenting your progress concerning your plan, you are calmly and logically keeping the plan going.

You can have stress work *for you* and not against you. Life's stressors and setbacks could galvanize you into action to make some changes. When making your plan and sticking to it, keep these things in mind (Powell, 1992):

- Try to think of setbacks not as defeats, but as reasons for change. Look at what you have done improperly and correct it.

- Think of stress as an energizer where new demands are a challenge, no matter how difficult. For example, a job reassignment from the jail to the courts at first may seem difficult. Look on it instead as a new phase in your career, and a chance to learn a new skill. You can put this skill on your professional resume.

- Rather than asking, "What is the worst possible outcome?" or "This [a negative thing] is going to happen," ask, "What is the best thing that may happen?"

125

- Take a break and pause between the stressors. Rest and recuperate before taking on something else. For example, after a difficult day checking some uncooperative clients in the field, rest before tackling that difficult report for the judge.

- Remember, you are the boss. You cannot control other people's actions. If they "fly off the handle," so be it. You can control how you react and respond to stressors. You manage your own emotions. Do not try to please everyone—you cannot. Try to please yourself.

- Look ahead past the stressful times at the long-range picture. Try not to think day-to-day, but months ahead at your goals.

Physical Wellness

One of the central themes throughout this book has been the importance of maintaining good physical health through proper diet and exercise. Not only does it help physically, but a healthy eating regimen and regular exercise help us mentally, too. It allows us to relax more easily, feel better about ourselves, and clear our minds.

What do we mean when we say we should be physically fit? To be physically fit, one must perform activities, such as exercise that bring out the following three results (Charlesworth and Nathan, 1984):

- Cardio-respiratory endurance: the capacity of our heart and lungs to withstand strenuous activities for long periods of time (twenty to thirty minutes in duration)

- Flexibility: the ability to move our bodies from one extreme position to another, such as bending from the waist to touch our feet or turning at the waist to the side

- Muscular function: muscular strength, endurance, and power—how strong we are, how we resist muscle fatigue, and how strong and fast force can be applied

An exercise program should support a goal of reaching a fitness level in these three areas. Also, it should be on a schedule or regular timetable of exercises. This can be difficult to do, however, if you work long hours or are on shift work. If that is the case, you must try to fit in an exercise schedule as best you can, even if it is only twenty or thirty minutes a day, three times a week. Anything you can do is better than nothing. Use time management to make the time to exercise. For example, instead of watching the news while sprawled out on the couch after work every day, use the time to work out on a rowing machine or a stationary bicycle, or do calisthenics while watching television. Instead of taking the elevator, walk up the flights of stairs.

Some of us put up mental barriers to exercise. Pain is one. When exercising, we must warm up and cool down or start slowly and increase the frequency of the exercise gradually. Expense is another common reason why people do not exercise. Joining a spa or health club can be expensive. However, many community centers offer fitness rooms, gyms (with basketball and volleyball courts), and swimming pools that are both inexpensive and convenient. You might want to consider buying your own exercise equipment. Some exercise machines are inexpensive and portable. A good book on exercises you can do at home costs just a few dollars. *See* for example, Pearson's *More than Muscle: A Total Fitness Program for Corrections and Law Enforcement* (2000) that is available from the American Correctional Association.

Boredom is another barrier, but varying the exercise activity can eliminate that obstacle. Exercising with a spouse or friend also will make the activity less tedious. Watch a movie or favorite television program or listen to music while exercising.

People often say, "I'm just too pooped." Do not fall into that rut. If you are tired after a hard day and feel that swimming a half-mile is too much, at least take a walk, or do something active. Appendix B offers basic information on exercising that will help you get started.

Coping with Shift Work

A serious threat to physical wellness is the strain of shift work. Throughout history, human beings adapted to working during the day and sleeping at night. However, society and technology have changed. With more demands on industry and the human services professions, more people work evening and midnight shifts. Correctional workers, such as prison and jail officers, often have to work shifts. The rate of workers on shift work has grown almost 1 percent a year since World War II. More than one-fourth of all working men and a sixth of all working women work rotating shifts. This translates into 21 million Americans (Moore-Ede, 1983). Today, according to the National Sleep Foundation, more than 22 million Americans work shifts from hospital workers to cab drivers to law enforcement personnel, including correctional staff (Medstar, 2004).

Shift work can be a stressor because human beings have a natural, biological need for sleep, with adults typically needing approximately eight to eight and a half hours of sleep per night (Medstar, 2004). Our bodies have biological clocks built in that tell us when to go to sleep, eat, get up, and so on. This biological clock can adjust an hour or two each day, but cannot adjust quickly to an eight- or twelve-hour change on rotating shifts. The negative effects of shift work are digestive disorders, sleep disorders, and disruptions in family and social life.

How can we positively cope with shift work and promote a feeling of wellness? Try the following suggestions (Moore-Ede, 1983; Pfeiffer and Webster, 1992):

1. Work on improving your sleep. Prepare for the midnight shift by staying up late and then sleep in late for a few days before midnight shifts. This will help you adjust to working all night. Your alertness will increase. Avoid loud music, caffeine, alcohol, tobacco, heavy exercise, and stressful situations at least three hours before going to bed. Use your bed for sleeping, not for watching television or eating snacks.

2. Use the light/dark cycle. Your biological clock says sleep when it is dark. Make the room where you sleep as dark as possible by using thick drapes or blinds. When you get up, make the room bright with light. This will tell your biological clock that you should be awake. Sleep for only eight-hour periods of time, and try to avoid napping.

3. Give yourself a proper sleeping environment. Make sure your bedroom or sleeping area is quiet and peaceful. The temperature should be comfortable. Some workers use a pleasant noise or hum such as a fan, a sound machine, or air conditioner to block out daytime street noises. Put a pillow over the phone or turn down the ringer. Let an answering machine pick up the calls. Keep your bedroom at a cool, constant nighttime temperature.

4. Develop a relaxing bedtime routine, such as taking a hot bath or shower, listening to music or reading.

5. Watch your diet. Until your body adjusts to a different shift, avoid greasy, starchy, or heavy foods. Eat light foods, such as fruit, salads, soups, or toast. This will be easier on your digestive system as well as your weight-control program. About an hour before bedtime, have a glass of warm milk and a high carbohydrate snack such as a whole grain muffin or toast.

6. Have an agreement with your family. Make sure they understand the rigors of shift work. Plan family activities so they will not conflict with your sleep time. Ask your neighbors, too, to be considerate and repay their kindness.

Mental Wellness

You must feel well mentally to handle stress. Relaxation is an important aspect to handling stress. However, there are several other components you should include in your stress-management plan, such as acceptance, a core philosophy, career goals, maintaining distance, vacations, religion, education, humor, a "monastery" approach (which will be explained later), hobbies, decreasing worry, and possibly a job change. We will look at each of these ways to handle stress.

Acceptance

You must learn to accept the fact that this is not a perfect world. Perfect worlds do not exist. Do not ask, "Why can't inmates or clients do what they are told?" Accept the fact that offenders live a different lifestyle than you. One jail officer notes that if offenders did not act the way they do, corrections professionals would not have jobs. At home, remember that life itself is stress—how we handle its effects is what counts.

Core Philosophy

Many of us have different philosophies about the field of corrections and stress. If you have a negative philosophy, such as "this job is a hassle" or "all this job is good for is to pay the bills," you will look at your whole career as a stressor. Your underlying or "core" philosophy should be positive.

Career Goals

What do you want out of your career? Some correctional officers want to move up the ladder quickly. Everyone wants to be promoted—more pay, better working conditions, and better benefits are inviting. However, you can stress yourself out if you stake your total well being on getting a promotion. Not everyone who wants to be promoted will be. And if you are not promoted, feelings of unworthiness and getting nowhere after years of service and effort begin to surface. Work can become meaningless (Hill, 1991). There are other things to enjoy in life that are not job-related. Also, if you find yourself "stuck" in the same job over a long period of time and you are feeling frustrated and angry, consider your options. You can ask for a transfer, get specialized training, or objectively look at why you are not being promoted. Then, take steps to improve your situation. Do you need to improve your appearance? Would training help?

Developing Positive Self-Talk

Your inner dialog has a big effect on how you perceive the world around you. The following positive self-talks and philosophies help these workers keep calm and reduce their stress and anger:

- "Avoid letting inmates notice you are anxious, under stress, or feeling tense about a given situation. Remain calm and collected and by all means, respond professionally; this will help you handle stress on the job and perform in the best interest of maintaining security." *Jail Officer*

- "I guess my own solution to stress is my drive through the country, going to work and coming home. It brings peace. It helps, too, to leave the problems of the job with the job." *Juvenile Counselor*

- "I have found two ways to conquer stress that work for me. One is to leave problems at the gate. No matter what sort of critical situation arises on the job to cause tension, I try to never take the problem home. The other alternative is to find something to occupy my off-duty time that is relaxing and satisfying." *Probation Officer*

- "Knowing how to be flexible and change from one thought to the other, one issue to the other, or one crisis to the other can be quite helpful . . . because of the clientele a probation officer is involved with, emergencies come up on a day-to-day basis. Knowing how to put things in perspective, prioritizing issues, and having a level head all help in alleviating stress factors." *Correctional Officer*

One correctional officer has a good philosophy. First, his basic motto is that he has to like what he does. Second, if he does not get promoted, he makes the best of his situation. Third, he considers any transfer or new assignment a challenge and considers anything that improves his job a promotion in itself.

Maintaining Distance

Part of your strategy should be to keep your distance from offenders. This is especially true in the probation and parole field. Probation officers who become overly involved with their clients take on the role of counselor/therapist instead of being more objective and making offenders take on responsibility. This conflict between the "counselor's" view and the probation officer's view can become emotionally stressful.

Other studies also have found that helpers, such as probation officers, who get too emotionally involved with troubled offenders, undergo stress. To avoid this trap, probation officers may distance themselves too much. The trick is to find a middle ground where probation or correctional officers are close enough to empathize and assist, but far enough away to be objective (Hill, 1991).

Vacations

Not taking a vacation is detrimental to your stress-management plan. You may feel uncomfortable taking a two-week vacation, and you may wonder who will handle your job responsibilities while you are away. Despite your doubts, you still should take vacations. To calm your fears, consider the following points:

1. **Do not think of yourself as indispensable.** Other workers can fill in for you, and in time, you can fill in for them when they want to take vacations. The jail, prison, or probation office will go on without you.

2. **Plan your vacation.** Let your supervisor know well in advance. A few weeks before your vacation, start thinking of projects and tasks to be done or delegated. Give yourself a "cushion." For example, if a report is due on Friday and your two-week vacation starts Saturday, have the report done by Tuesday or Wednesday. That way, if the report is returned for revisions, you will have a few days to do it and still avoid a last-minute rush. At home, begin planning early. Do not wait until the last minute to pack. Make checklists and follow them. Vacations should be filled with good stress—not bad.

3. **Use some of your stress-management skills.** Plan to exercise when on vacation so you will not get stressed out over a weight gain. Use time management and organizing skills to pack, plan your activities, and so on.

For example, Keith, a sergeant in a work-release center, and his wife and two children planned a trip to Disney World in Florida. Things were busy at work and at home with last minute packing, staff meetings, and a host of other details. When he left work that Friday afternoon, he thought of the fun they would have in Florida. But on the way to the airport, Keith wondered if he had taken care of all the "loose ends" at work. He remembered one thing: a monthly training meeting while he would be away. He wondered: does the staff know? He had forgotten to put out a memorandum. Because he was the staff training coordinator, it was his responsibility. On the plane he worried about it. Although he knew his family would get angry if he called his work, the next morning, while his children were asleep and his wife was in the shower, he called the center and talked to his corporal. His corporal advised him that the staff knew about the meeting. When his wife caught him on the telephone, she was upset and reminded him that he was on vacation. Through this experience, he learned to plan ahead and to delegate if he could not get to every loose end.

Religion

Some individuals find that being active in a religious group is beneficial. No matter what your faith, involvement in church, synagogue, temple, or mosque lets you do positive things while at the same time meeting people outside of law enforcement. Religious activities can help you guard against viewing people negatively. After working in an environment filled with negative emotions, it is mentally refreshing to be involved with something good.

Education

Part of your personalized plan should be education. Instead of focusing on job aspects that cause you stress and lead to burnout, you can exercise your mind by obtaining knowledge. Learning cannot only be refreshing mentally, but it can serve as a distraction to negative thoughts. Many workers may think that education means going back to college. For some who have goals of entering different areas of corrections, this may be the way to go. If you do not wish to go back to college or cannot afford it, there are other ways to obtain knowledge, such as reading books on corrections, taking correspondence courses offered by organizations such as the American Correctional Association (ACA), and reading training materials from ACA, the American Jail Association, and other organizations for correctional workers. You also can attend training seminars offered by law enforcement academies, mental health organizations, and other professional organizations. If you are not interested in pursuing a college degree, keep in mind that you can attend college classes without being part of a degree program. Also, check out what training is available online, which may fit your schedule.

Humor

It is good to laugh. Laughing makes you feel better. Correctional workers often have a unique sense of humor. They tend to laugh at "odd" offenders and they enjoy playing jokes. Humor can take the "edge" off stress, and laughter helps to defuse stressful situations and events, such as the tense moments immediately after a cellblock fight. The stress is over, one officer says something humorous, and the others laugh. Facial muscles relax when we laugh, and laughter also signals the body to switch off the stress/emergency alarm system (Witkin-Lanoil, 1986). One corrections supervisor said:

> *"I transferred into a new section after being out of jail operations for eight years. I was worried: how would the new staff take to me? Could we work together? I could have walked in that first day all nervous and edgy. However, some harmless practical jokes were pulled on me, and some of the officers cracked some witticisms. I laughed right along with them. The atmosphere eased a lot and I knew that I had been accepted."*

A Monastery Approach

Throughout history, monasteries have been places of refuge, silence, and peace. When you think of a monastery, you think of a place where you can get away from it all. This method of stress management advocates silence, reflection, and calmness—

in other words, relaxation. Days in the park with music or a good book, a weekend at a quiet inn or resort, and a quiet hike in the woods, are all monastery approaches. People who use this method to unwind report that they feel serene, energized, and less tense or wound up (Engeler, 1993). These feelings can be obtained if you use a little imagination and create your own monastery.

Hobbies

Hobbies can be a real charge to your drained mental state and having one is a good stress reliever. Hobbies can be any activity that interests you or makes you feel good: woodworking, sewing, stamp or coin collecting, refinishing furniture, painting, gardening, reading, playing a musical instrument, or cooking. Do not let everything in your life be related to work.

Decreasing Worry

Worry can be very draining on you emotionally. Correctional workers have to worry about security, safety, and a myriad of other things, both on and off the job. If you find yourself overwhelmed with worry, stop and take a deep breath and relax. Plan a strategy to deal with your worries. Although as adults we have responsibilities and therefore must be concerned about certain things in our lives, being relaxed and taking action about problems is better than just worrying about them.

Sometimes we worry about something that might happen and we get worked up. Mark Twain knew what he was speaking of when he said, "Troubles are only mental; it is the mind that manufactures them, and the mind can gorge them, banish them, abolish them….it has never been my way to bother much about things which you can't cure" (www.twainquotes.com).

A coworker asked one veteran jail officer who had been on the job for twenty-five years what he had learned. The veteran replied that he had learned various ways to handle situations and problems. Also, this had led to a feeling of inner strength. As a result, he had learned not to worry, saying that he worries a lot less about things than he did earlier in his career. He also had a self-motto that was taken from some advice that a jail mental-health therapist had told him: Worry is the interest you pay on a debt that may never come due.

Job Change

Changing your job is a drastic strategy. Some workers get out of the field because they cannot deal with the stress. The stress of working in corrections may have cost some their health, mental well-being, marriage, or relationship. There is no shame in changing jobs, but if you do, think it out thoroughly, talk it over with your family, and ask yourself if it will be a change for the better. Maybe you should redesign your stress-management plan or ask for a transfer to a new area. Give it a lot of thought and do what you believe is best for you.

Family Support

Family support is important to a stress-reduced lifestyle. Traditionally, hearth and home have been viewed as a welcome sight to a tired worker after a long day. Your home and family should be an island of calm in a sea of stress.

However, a family in itself is a stressor. Some stressors, such as births, deaths, arguments between family members, divorce, marriage, buying a new home, starting school, and moving are contributing factors to "primary family stress." Another way to look at primary family stress is to think of stressors or problems that start within the family unit. Secondary family stress include stressors that come from outside the family, such as frustrations, anger, and coldness resulting from working in corrections (Benson et al., 1987).

No family is perfect. The television shows of the 1950s and 1960s portrayed nice, neat families who lived in houses that looked like homes in magazines. Problems were trivial, and there was always a happy ending. No one ever seemed to get tired or irritable. Mothers stayed home, and fathers worked regular hours. But things are different in real life.

Friends can be a strong means of support to the correctional worker. Correctional officers often socialize with other correctional workers. They find solace and support in each other because they share the same job-related problems and the same perspective on those problems. However, good friends, both inside and outside of corrections, can supply advice, humor, wholesome activity, and emotional support, just like family. Although it is normal to have a lot of friends in the corrections field, friends outside of corrections can provide a refreshing outlook on life.

Both correctional workers and their families can help limit the amount of stress a correctional worker feels. There are several important things that workers and their families can do to effectively cope with stress:

1. Family members should know what stress is and what it does and recognize when someone in the family is under stress.

2. Family members should participate in positive-coping techniques, such as recreation and exercise. This can be done individually or together.

3. Family members should have a "calm down" period after work, school, or household chores. Parents in a dual-career family should give each other thirty minutes of relaxation time after work, during which problems and concerns cannot be brought up.

4. Family members should encourage open communication with each other. In an "on the go" household, some families use the dinner hour to talk to one another. Talking is important, but so is listening. If a family member is stressed out, he or she should be allowed to talk about the stress. Other family members should listen and give feedback. Family members should not try to "top" each other's stress. Discuss the stressors one at a time, listen, and give support and advice.

5. Families should encourage workers to take time off and take vacations.

6. Family members should make birthdays, anniversaries, and holidays special.

7. Each family member should make a special effort to show one another he or she is appreciated.

8. Workers and their families should be aware of negative-coping techniques and if they are present, work to eliminate them.

9. Workers and their spouses should improve, if necessary, their lifestyle by focusing on diet, exercise, time management, and leisure.

10. Workers and their spouses should examine how they come across to other family members. If the answer is unpleasant, do something about it.

11. Workers should sincerely compliment family members as much as possible. Comments such as "your report card was great," "that meal was delicious," and "the house looks great" are always welcome. Family members should learn to reciprocate.

12. Workers must leave their jobs at work. Keep your work life and family life separate. If you are called in on overtime or have to work extra hours, do not just promise to make it up to the spouse or family. Do it!

Communication is the key. Family members and significant others and the worker must talk to each other about the stress. If these steps do not work and the stress level in your home is not decreasing, seek outside help. There are several ways you or your spouse can do this. First, if your agency has an Employee Assistance Program (EAP), see the EAP counselor. The counselor may be able to provide short-term counseling or refer you to a marriage or family counselor. Consult a member of your faith. A pastoral counseling service may offer help. Or seek out community organizations that can help.

Abundance

Finally, look at your life and see how abundantly rich you are. Some of us want to be stress free by having monetary wealth or material things. Money can act like a wound in our lives, and we bandage it by buying things, sometimes spending beyond our means. Abundance is more than monetary wealth and material things. It is the following:

- Health

- Positive relationships: family, friends, people who we like

- Good ideas: the excitement in change and trying to do things better and improve our lives

- Talent: recognizing the special things that we are capable of doing

- Spirituality: Knowing that our lives are special and part of the larger plan, according to our faith

If you strive to obtain these things, then you will have abundance in your life (DeWitt, 2003).

A personalized plan takes a lot of thought, effort, and commitment. Through your personalized strategy, you can learn that life is good and does not have to be cut short because of a career in corrections.

Stress and Crisis

By reading this chapter, you should understand the following:

- The nature of stress-induced crisis and critical incidents

- What posttraumatic stress syndrome is and its effects on correctional staff

- What resources are available to staff, such as peer counseling, critical-incident stress debriefing, employee assistance programs, and agency programs

While the main theme of this book has been to present preventative measures to offset the destructive nature of stress in corrections, the problem of what to do in a crisis must be explored. Depending on the job assignment, how well the agency is managed and personal stress-management techniques, some correctional workers experience less stress than others and may deal with it in a positive way. For example, in a prison, a counselor may experience different stressors than a correctional officer who works the disciplinary unit. A probation office may have a proactive director who requires that her staff-clerks, probation officers, and others receive periodic stress-management training. Supervisors may or may not practice the management techniques discussed in Chapter 6. A sheriff in one jail may go to roll calls and actively support peer counseling and EAP programs, while in the next county, the sheriff takes little or no action about stress in his jail.

This chapter will discuss what to do in a crisis, when all of the stress-management efforts have appeared to fail, and a correctional worker may feel that he or she is at the end of the line. Each of us is different. The breaking point for one person may not be the breaking point for another.

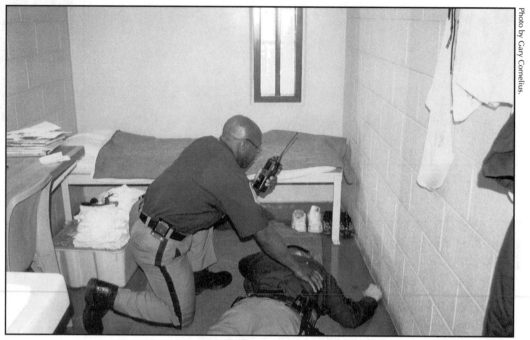

Seeing a co-worker or friend injured on the job is a major stressor.

Stress-Induced Crisis: Critical Incidents

The dictionary defines a crisis as a "decisive or crucial moment," or a "sudden change for better or worse in the course of an acute illness." This definition can be applied to our discussion of stress management.

A decisive or crucial moment, or what some of us call a *critical incident*, could be when we feel that the job has gotten us nowhere, we cannot take it anymore, or that we cannot put up with _____. The blank can be filled in by any of the stressors that we face on or off the job. It is like a "spark" that launches us into negative feelings and emotions.

For example, a prison officer witnesses an inmate brutally stabbing another—right out of the blue, directly in front of him. A jail officer discovers an inmate hanging dead at 3 a.m. A client attacks the probation officer in her office after she counsels him not to miss any more drug screenings or he will be violated. A drug-crazed teenager who has been brought into detention spits on a juvenile worker.

At home, it could be when the wife says that she has had enough and walks out, taking the children. It could be when an officer stumbles home drunk and sees the service weapon in his drawer and thinks that tonight he will end it.

The public may view law enforcement officers, including correctional officers, as strong types who are supposed be strong instead of weak, are not to feel emotions, and must hold a steady course. In reality, both police and correctional officers deal with traumatic stressors and events, sometimes so frequently that they seem overwhelming. The following enumeration lists some of the traumatic things that those in corrections face (Monta, 2002):

- Life-threatening situations that involve offenders and criminals who are armed with deadly weapons, such as guns, knives, homemade weapons, and so forth

- Combative physical struggles with offenders/inmates to overcome resistance

- Serious on-duty, job-related injury or exposure to a serious illness, such as HIV, hepatitis C, or tuberculosis

- Situations that require split-second decisions on whether to use deadly force

- The responsibility and duty to make an arrest or act in a situation that can cause personal grief, anxiety, and/or disappointment—such as taking action against a fellow officer, family member, friend, or inmate with whom the officer has had a positive relationship

- Being on the scene, viewing work crime, accidents, and events such as shootings, stabbings, assaults, illnesses, and suicides

- Feeling heartbreaking empathy for victims of crime, accident victims, and innocent people who have been hurt

The stress caused by these events can pile up if not dealt with in a positive way, as discussed elsewhere in this book. Corrections work has been described as "boredom coupled with intermittent terror," and critical incidents can overwhelm our coping mechanisms (Davis, 1995). Things can happen very intensely and very fast.

For example, a disturbance erupts in a prison recreation yard. The tower officer looks down, reaches for his rifle, and fires a warning shot. The inmates immediately quiet down. When the relief tower officer arrives at the top of the tower, he has to physically pry the rifle from the tower officer's hands. Or, at 7: 00 a.m., the tier officer lets the inmates out of their cells for breakfast. While the inmates are lining up, a fight starts, and an inmate cuts off another inmate's ear using a folded can cover. The inmate who is cut falls to the floor with blood spurting everywhere from his ear wound and a neck wound. Backup officers arrive and see the tier officer just standing there. They activate his personal alarm and take charge of the situation. The tier officer cannot move (Davis, 1995).

If these officers do not talk to anyone or deal with this stress, it will eat at them repeatedly. This is not good for their personal lives, their professional lives, or their health.

Post-Traumatic Stress Disorder

Much has been discussed and written about post-traumatic stress disorder, or PTSD. The basic definition of PTSD states "it is the mind and body's reoccurring psychological and physical responses to a highly stressful event from the recent or distant past." Another way to look at it is "shell shock"—the battle is over, but the effects go on and on (Albrecht, 1999; Pranzo and Pranzo, 1999).

For example, a correctional officer breaks up a fight and is knocked unconscious. A female probation officer is attacked during a home visit. The effects of the stress—the anxiety and fear are still there. The physical and psychological feelings can range from mild and not severe, to irritability, to severe to the point of incapacitation. Sometimes the feelings and images are so strong that the correctional worker may feel and see them in daydreams or nightmares. They never seem to go away (Albrecht, 1999; Pranzo and Pranzo, 1999).

The negative-coping mechanisms can "kick in." To decrease the effects of these feelings, workers may become withdrawn. They may get quiet in an effort to make it all go away. They may say to themselves that the event wasn't anything to worry about, it was no big deal, and "I can handle it"—while all the while they are having nightmares about that hostage situation when they were grabbed or they see that inmate who they knew and was helping through a crisis hanging dead from a shower rod with bugged-out eyes and a stretched neck.

While PTSD triggers responses in which the person relives the event or situation, workers will try to avoid it. They

- may try to avoid thoughts, feelings, or conversations associated with the traumatic event
- may try to avoid people or places associated with the trauma
- find they are unable to remember an important detail or aspect of the trauma
- show a markedly diminished interest or participation in important activities
- may feel detached or estranged from others
- may show a restricted range of emotion or affect, such as not showing love or affection for others
- may think that they have a short-term future, such as not having a career, children, a long marriage, or living a normal lifespan to retirement

(Long, 2003)

Signs of persistent PTSD include sleep difficulties, such as falling or staying asleep; irritability or having angry outbursts; having trouble concentrating; hypervigilance; and exaggerated startle responses (Long, 2003). Mental health professionals consider the PTSD chronic if such symptoms last longer than three months. From one to three months, the PTSD is considered acute. Sometimes the PTSD is considered delayed if it appears several months or years after the event. It is not exactly known why some people do not suffer from PTSD, experience acute PTSD, or fall victim to chronic or delayed PTSD. Factors that may influence this may be how severe the trauma was, how many times the person was exposed to trauma, how close the person was to the event, if negative reactions are received by others, if the trauma was inflicted from others, and how dangerous it was perceived to be (Foa, Davidson, Frances, and Ross, 1999).

Staff operations are affected as the officer frequently calls in sick, or comes to work bleary eyed from lack of sleep. The person with PTSD may become irritable on the job and snap at colleagues. Transfer requests may increase, and officers may become inpatient when they cannot transfer quickly to other jobs. Family life suffers as the officer sinks into depression, or jumps at a loud noise, reliving the night of the jail riot. He may see someone who looks like the inmate who grabbed him. Nights are turned into tossing-and-turning sessions complete with nightmares and sweats. Management also has to deal with all of this fallout. Now, several key questions arise: If critical incident stress can lead to posttraumatic stress disorder, is there any hope? And—what can a worker do? The answers are "yes" and "plenty." The help includes the following:

- peer counseling
- critical incident stress debriefing
- employee assistance programs (EAPs)
- agency programs

Peer Counseling

Peer counseling means what it says—fellow workers who are specially trained in stress counseling. As a result of their background, they assist coworkers who are having a tough time with stress. There are advantages for the stressed-out worker to seek peer counseling (Carr, 2003):

- A peer worker will understand what the victimized officer is going through, especially if he or she has experienced a similar event.
- Peer counselors convince the officers that they are not alone. In fact, the ideal candidates for peer counselors are level-headed people, who staff seems to

trust, talk openly to, or see or seek advice from in an emergency. They have a good reputation in the agency. New staff should be informed that if a traumatic event happens to them or the stress of corrections gets too much for both the home and work fronts, the peer counseling team will help them cope.

- A crisis in corrections often is disruptive to the natural-support system, such as the family. A worker can say, "Everything will be OK because my family is there for me." However, when he gets home, the stressor, such as an injury or hostage crisis can be the family's worst nightmare, and they may have trouble dealing with it. They may be more traumatized than the officer, and he/she has to cope with this, possibly along with this stress of the event and pleadings to "quit the job." Or, the family may be undergoing its own crisis and do not have the emotional energy to expend on the correctional crises.

An effective peer counselor has the ability to listen, clarify what the officer is feeling, and offer support. A key trait is the peer counselor resisting the temptation to give advice, such as saying "if I were you, I would" (Carr, 2003). This is what caring friends do, but their primary job is to give support.

Using peer counselors has both benefits and limitations. Besides being less expensive than professional mental health professionals, peer counselors have "instant credibility" because the stressed-out officer feels that they are empathetic. Officers who are reluctant to open up to a mental health professional may talk to a peer counselor. Peer counselors are available because they work at the same place, and can recommend the stress program to others. Limitations include the propensity to offer counseling that they are not trained to do; they are not qualified mental health professionals. Some officers may feel that peer counselors will not keep conversations confidential and would rather talk to a qualified professional. By not performing properly and ethically, peer counselors can open themselves, the program, and the agency up to legal liability (Finn, 2000).

Critical-Incident Stress Debriefing

For the correctional worker to get through the stress of a traumatic event, a debriefing is crucial. In most cases, the workers must go back to work in the same environment (Finn, 2000). The probation officer must go back to doing home visits after a client grabbed her or she walked in on a domestic argument and was assaulted. The juvenile worker must go back into the detention center among the same juvenile offender population that caused a disturbance.

Anecdotal evidence from the field, rather than scientific study, supports the view that stress debriefings help some officers and workers who have experienced traumatic stress obtain some emotional relief. There are other benefits (Finn, 2000):

- Debriefings may alleviate and relieve inappropriate feelings of guilt. For example, an officer responds to the trouble call of another officer across the recreation yard. Inmates seriously injure the officer in trouble, and the responding officer may feel that he was too slow, when his supervisors feel that he did all he could. A debriefing may help him to realize that he is not to blame. One debriefing officer conducted six debriefings after a major prison riot a few years ago. Dispatchers at the prison felt helpless because they heard what was happening and could do nothing. The other officers gave them "terrific support" to relieve their feelings of guilt.

- Stress or critical-incident debriefings can quash rumors and speculation based on conjecture and not fact. In debriefings, staff can get a fuller picture of what actually happened instead of what someone thought happened.

- Debriefings demonstrate in a clear way that the administration actually cares. Good supervisors actually care about the line staff. However, there is a comfort zone among line staff and the traditional boundary between line staff and supervisors. Many rank and file workers feel that the "brass" should not be around when debriefings are taking place.

There are other key points to remember about peer counseling and stress debriefing. In serious situations, an agency investigation (by the well-known internal affairs), a criminal investigation, court action, grand jury, and the media can keep the trauma "alive" to the worker. Also, colleagues, friends, and family all want to hear what happened, but not how it has affected the worker. Colleagues may want the stressed-out workers to say that they will be okay. "Armchair quarterbacks or generals" may criticize the worker, saying that he or she should have done this or that, or they would have done things differently (Carr, 2003).

Employee Assistance Program (EAP)

While the benefits of the Employee Assistance Programs (EAPs) have been discussed in detail in Chapter 6, EAP counselors' usefulness to the stressed-out worker cannot be overstated. EAPs are staffed by trained professionals who can throw the stressed-out worker a lifeline. While peer counselors and critical-stress debriefings can serve to alleviate the emotional pain, guilt, and negativity associated with stress, EAP counselors can delve deeper into the worker's stress and deal with its causes. Also, as qualified and licensed staff, they can make the proper and effective referrals to other mental health personnel.

Pennsylvania Department of Corrections

In the Pennsylvania Department of Corrections (DOC), for example, the slogan is "Minimize Your Stress, Maximize Yourself." In a department of approximately 13,000 employees, a twenty-year employee is looked on as a valuable million-dollar investment. The agency offers to employees and families the services of the State Employee Assistance Program (SEAP). Also, there is a departmentwide Critical Incident Stress Management (CISM) at each correctional facility. Employees who feel that they have experienced a traumatic event are encouraged to contact the chief psychologist or CISM team leader at their facility directly.

Stress Programs of Agencies

An agency stress program is one of the best ways that the "top brass" and managers of an agency can show all correctional workers and their families that they do care about the effect of job stress. Agency-stress programs advocate the use of peer counselors, critical-incident stress debriefings, EAPs, and family involvement. Many programs use a combination of in-house personnel, such as staff-peer counselors, and contracted-outside personnel such as local mental-health service providers. Stress programs have many benefits (Finn, 2000):

- They save correctional administrators money through the reduction of overtime to cover for staff on sick leave or from staff quitting. When workers are traumatized or burned out, a common coping mechanism is to call in sick or quit. Someone has to work the post. Overtime is expensive.

- They improve officer performance by enhancing morale and causing workers to have a better mental outlook and physical well being. Workers feel better and look better.

- They increase facility safety due to reduced distractions, boredom, and complacency caused by stress. By reducing complacency, staff pay more attention to security, and all staff, visitors, and inmates benefit.

- These programs improve relations between management and officer/worker labor unions.

- They demonstrate concern for the employees. As one supervisor in a state prison system observed, in cases of an accident or an assault when an officer is hospitalized, a stress-program staff member is there to be sure that the officer is cared for and the family is contacted and assisted. A paramilitary organization can get impersonal, and a stress program shows that the agency cares about its employees.

In the past several years, the National Institute of Justice (NIJ) has awarded police and correctional agencies grants to implement stress-reduction programs through the Corrections and Law Enforcement Family Support (CLEFS) Program. Since 1996, the National Institute of Justice has awarded thirty-two CLEFS Program Grants to law enforcement agencies, including corrections (NIJ, 2003). While these grants are for fixed periods of time, they serve to plant seeds throughout the agency for managing stress and caring about staff and their families. These seeds are trained peer counselors, educated staff, enlightened family members, and supervisors who realize what their subordinates go through.

A study by the National Institute of Justice found that most correctional officers feel that organizational factors, not the dangers of correctional work, were their greatest source of stress. Not only is stress on the job a concern, but so is stress at home. Of the correctional officers' spouses surveyed, 50 percent reported stress from their spouse's workplace, such as critical incidents, poor communication of rules, and changing rules or inconsistent rules at their spouse's workplace. Other stressors are lack of recognition and underappreciation for their spouse by the agency and concern

The Rhode Island Centurion Program

Calling itself a program that treats the "heart behind the badge," for the past twenty-five years, the Centurion Stress Unit has provided trained staff who have responded to requests for help from criminal justice professionals and family members following lethal-force encounters, civil disasters, fatalities, injuries to staff and colleagues, tactical missions, or correctional disorders. The program serves the criminal justice communities, police and corrections, in Rhode Island and Southeastern Massachusetts. On-site support and after-incident assistance is provided. The following are provided at no cost:

- critical-incident stress debriefing, including follow-up support for staff and families

- stress-management education, both for recruits and in-service within the Rhode Island Municipal Police Academy and the Rhode Island Department of Corrections Training Center. This training is provided by the Centurion staff and staff from Butler Hospital, the only private psychiatric and substance abuse hospital in Rhode Island. The hospital works closely with the Centurion program and sponsors the activities of the Centurion Critical Incident Stress Team.

- in-service training is offered onsite at the requesting agency and is customized to fit the agency's specific needs. Centurion and Butler staff provide the training.

- stress-unit development: A consultant is available to criminal justice agencies, on site upon request, for the development of operational stress-unit guidelines.

The Centurion System program has proven very effective and has received recognition from the National Institute of Justice in 1997 as a regional stress-management resource for criminal justice agencies. A Centurion affiliate, the Stress Management Unit of the Rhode Island Department of Corrections, was recognized in 1999 as a National Model Program for its addressing stressors that are unique in the corrections field.

Two incidents illustrate the good work that has been done by this program, which is supported by the United Way, other charities, third-party reimbursements, direct client fees, and endowment interest (Finn, 2000):

In 1997, a riot occurred at the Rhode Island maximum-security correctional facility. Five officers were injured. The supervisor of the hostage-negotiating team paged John Carr, Centurion Director, who in turn contacted Mark Messier, the stress-unit coordinator and a correctional officer. Officer Messier activated the program's peer counselors and responded to the scene with John Carr. Director Carr and Officer Messier contacted the officers' family members and had them meet near the facility, but not at the incident site. A peer supporter was on hand to talk one-on-one with the family members. After the officers were released, a peer rode with each of the officers in the ambulance and remained with them at the hospital. John Carr and his wife, Patricia, a peer supporter and a social worker, conducted a debriefing for the family members two weeks after the incident. Why? Many husbands and wives were concerned and worried about whether their spouses should go back into the facility. One couple asked for further assistance and the Carrs went into their home to provide further support. As a result of the concern and communication and the caring shown by this stress program, none of the five officers resigned.

The Carrs also introduce the peer counselors to the officers' families at academy family night at the graduation of an academy class. They talk to the families and tell them that this is a good resource. John says: "….the academy is training them [officers] to be lean, mean fighting machines just when I'm trying to tell them it's OK to feel afraid and come for help. As a result, I put a peer supporter in front of them who is a member of the cell-extraction team or a 199-pound maximum-security officer so the recruits can say to themselves, " That tactically trained person is a touchy feely peer?!"

For further information, contact:

John J. Carr, DCSW
Director
Family Service Society
33 Summer Street
Pawtucket, RI 02860
401-723-2124

Southeast Iowa Correctional Family Program

This program, funded by CLEFS, consists of four components: wellness, family support, and both supervisor and correctional officer in-service training. A wellness event provided education for staff and their families on sources of stress and how to get help. Two health fairs were conducted in which the warden of the Iowa State Penitentiary and the superintendent of the Mt. Pleasant Correctional Facility invited the families of staff. These programs featured nationally known guest speakers, fitness providers, hospitals, nutritionists, and counselors. Informational booths and children's activities were also present. The Wellness Challenge encouraged staff to learn about healthy lifestyles through challenges in physical activities, nutrition, personal health, mental health, and health-status improvement. All staff was invited to take part in a motivational program complete with pre- and post-challenge health screenings, measuring improvements in body composition, blood pressure, cholesterol, stress, nutrition, and physical activity. Monthly health and wellness education sessions were offered along with self-care manuals.

The feedback from officers and their families who participated was positive. One said that her husband was given peace of mind about where she worked. Another spouse said that his wife felt better understanding the security of the correctional facility.

The family-support component consisted of a spouse academy, where husband-and-wife teams presented information on the recognition and impact of stress. The Employee Assistance Program also conducted training on the many resources available to help families of staff undergoing the effects of job stress.

Another component was the development of a peer-support program, which listens to officers under stress and provides appropriate referrals, when necessary.

Peer support programs were viewed as early-detection mechanisms to help correctional staff deal with personal and professional problems before these problems become more serious. A part of this peer-support group was the Emergency Staff Services (ESS) program that helps families during emergencies at the correctional facilities.

The last two components were the supervisor and correctional officer in-service training program. In-house staff was trained through a train-the-trainers' program to conduct training in stress management. Subjects included sessions on burnout, domestic violence, and the many faces of stress. Noteworthy is the fact that correctional supervisors at the facilities were required to attend annual training in workplace relationships, EAP, and the "Peace Institute," which talked about conflict resolution and strengthening working relationships. Other supervisory classes were on crisis management and survival skills for middle managers.

The conclusion reached by the program staff was that the program was built step by step to create a strong, flexible, foundation that recognizes the value of agency employees and helps them and their families deal with stress and its many effects. For more information, contact:

Marlene Koopman
Mt. Pleasant Correctional Facility
1200 East Washington
Mt. Pleasant, Iowa 52641
319-385-9511 extension: 2470 or 319-385-2891

Correctional Officer Stress Management: Albert C. Wagner Youth Correctional Facility

New Jersey Department of Corrections

Funded by the National Institute of Justice and CLEFS, this program incorporated the following components:

- in-service stress-management training for officers
- training for supervisors
- family orientation: the corrections family-training academy
- a comprehensive wellness component

One of the mottos used by this program is the proverbial "an ounce of prevention is worth a pound of cure." In the Wellness Component, health classes that addressed both men's and women's wellness issues were offered throughout the workday to make it more convenient for staff to attend. A health educator taught the program. Workshops, one hour in length, discussed these issues:

- managing high blood pressure
- managing cholesterol levels
- obtaining better nutrition
- managing your weight and diabetes
- quitting smoking and becoming aware of alcohol/drug abuse programs
- understanding women's health
- becoming physically fit, testing, and evaluation

Staff could pick the topic that interested them. A private health-care provider offered health screenings at no cost. Screenings were in the areas of health risk and health-status assessments. Other tests also included: blood pressure, blood sugar, cholesterol, and body composition. The provider offered training in stress-management techniques, psychological and mental health, and an orientation to resilience. Follow-up services were available in the wellness component to encourage staff to take advantage of the services offered.

An important part of the program was the mandatory component of in-service stress-management training for line officers and a separate, different focus on the curriculum for custody supervisors. The supervisors' curriculum discussed management styles and possible indicators of distress in officers. The comprehensive training provided information on the causes of correctional stress and what can be done to combat its negative effects. The project director (William Hepner) was responsible for the development and implementation of the components of the grant.

A Critical Incident Stress Management Program (CISM) for corrections officers and their families was developed providing peer support and debriefings. Goals of the CISM program are to encourage ventilation, to validate and normalize stress reactions, to encourage follow up and support, and to provide officers and their families with additional assistance through many different resources.

A Corrections Family Training Academy (CFTA) (called "Family Day") was offered several times during the year, providing support for families, stress-prevention education, critical-incident stress management, and prison tours for correctional officers' spouses and children ages sixteen and over. The staff felt that it is important for the families and children to see what their loved ones have to deal with. A committee of officers developed a video skit. Other topics included the nature of corrections work, chronic stress among officers, spouses and partners, what to expect after a critical incident, resilience, and domestic-violence information/resources. Experienced correctional officers and partners teach the program.

The New Jersey State Policeman's Benevolent Association State Correction Officer Local Chapter also supported this program. The union thought that the stress-management techniques in the corrections program could be beneficial to its members, stating that the quality of life gained could be extended throughout a professional career and into a long and prosperous retirement.

For more information, contact:

William Hepner
New Jersey Department of Corrections Training Academy
PO Box 438-Building 14 Camp Drive
c/o National Guard Training Center
Sea Girt, NJ 08750

about their spouse contracting diseases from inmates due to their close proximity and contact with them (Wells, 2003).

However, thanks to a concern from agencies about correctional workers and their families when it comes to stress, some programs are making headway in stress management. This trend of making stress resources available to staff is spreading. Since 1995, the Texas Department of Criminal Justice has had a stress-reduction and staff-support program. At every unit and with every duty shift, there is at least one staff volunteer who is a member of the Post Trauma Staff Support Unit—a unit designed to be a "first responder" to assist staff with stressful incidents (Gaseau, 2003). In Oregon, state law mandates peer counseling and confidentiality guidelines for emergency-service providers and law enforcement officers (Oregon statute Title 18, Chapter 181, Section 181.360). In the New Mexico Corrections Department, therapeutic discussion, counseling and follow up will serve to minimize stress-related reactions of corrections department personnel, including handling of distressing sights, sounds, and/or events through the Critical Incident Stress Debriefing process (New Mexico DOC Procedure CD-031300, 02/26/94).

In conclusion, there is much that an agency can do to help employees and their families manage stress before the stress unravels their health, well-being, and their lives. It takes some research, some effort, and caring.

Appendix

A Healthy Diet

As discussed in Chapter 4, maintaining a healthy diet is crucial to a stress-management plan. Eating nutritious, healthy foods and watching your weight help you stay healthy, feel better about yourself, and maintain your adaptive energy. Proper eating habits, when combined with exercise and relaxation, can help your body and mind stay tuned up to cope with stress. Having a healthy diet does not mean you have to eat "rabbit food" or starve yourself. It does mean you allow your body to benefit from foods that are good for you.

Schwiesow and Bauman reported in 1994 that 50 million Americans were on diets annually, spending $32 million. In 1999, Americans were spending $33 billion a year on diets rather than exercising (Stein, 1999). Take a look at yourself. Are you overweight? Would you like to trim down? The first step is to find your proper weight. Your doctor or agency medical-exam unit can help you. Develop a plan before starting a diet and exercise program. At least one large insurance provider will now pay for weight-loss services. Check with your health-insurance provider to see what is covered. You also should consult a physician before starting a diet if you meet any of the following criteria:

- have not exercised regularly or at all in the past
- are overweight
- have high blood pressure
- are diabetic
- have a heart condition
- are pregnant or are a nursing mother
- suffer from any condition requiring medical treatment
- have not had a physical examination in the past several years

New Food and Activity Guidance from the Government

The U.S. Department of Agriculture recently has unveiled new nutritional guidelines. They are located at MyPyramid.gov where you can assess your food intake and your physical activity. We suggest readers go to this site and individualize their food profiles based on the latest proper nutritional requirements, which are dependent on their activity level, age, and sex. This site contains a wealth of information and even a food and activity tracker designed to keep you healthy.

Also, much has been discussed about "low-carb" diets, in which the weight-loss theory is that we eat carbohydrates in foods ranging from bread to fruit. The carbohydrates are broken down into simple sugars that cause the pancreas to produce insulin. Insulin, the body's main energy regulator, allows the sugars to be used for energy. Excess sugars are stored as fat to be used later. Excess sugar in the body causes an overproduction of insulin. The excess sugars cannot be absorbed into the cells, so excess fat builds. By eating fewer carbohydrates, the insulin system begins to correct itself. Blood-sugar levels decrease; stored fat is used for energy, thus commencing weight loss. In low-carb diets, you eat fewer carbohydrates and more proteins and fats (Stein, 1999).

There has been much debate among health care and nutritionists as to what is the "right" diet. There are diet plans for every taste, lifestyle, and the amount of willpower. Before you decide to take charge of your health and eat properly, get educated and study much of the good information that is available. Some plans are as follows:

Low-carbohydrate diets: eat fewer "carbs" and balance that with proteins and fats

Combination or "combo" diets: eat proteins and nonstarchy carbohydrates together, so the food will not be stored as fat

Low fat: stay away from fat, and for a long healthy life, eat natural, whole foods such as fruits and vegetables to keep weight down

Low calorie: foods are given point values which you do not exceed, or eat no more than a certain percentage of carbohydrates.

Many physicians and dieticians are wary of the "low-carb" diets. They favor the revised food pyramid. They feel what is effective is healthy eating according to the pyramid, combined with a reduced calorie intake and an increase in exercise and

MyPyramid
STEPS TO A HEALTHIER YOU
MyPyramid.gov

GRAINS	VEGETABLES	FRUITS	MILK	MEAT & BEANS
GRAINS Make half your grains whole	**VEGETABLES** Vary your veggies	**FRUITS** Focus on fruits	**MILK** Get your calcium-rich foods	**MEAT & BEANS** Go lean with protein
Eat at least 3 oz. of whole-grain cereals, breads, crackers, rice, or pasta every day 1 oz. is about 1 slice of bread, about 1 cup of breakfast cereal, or 1/2 cup of cooked rice, cereal, or pasta	Eat more dark-green veggies like broccoli, spinach, and other dark leafy greens Eat more orange vegetables like carrots and sweetpotatoes Eat more dry beans and peas like pinto beans, kidney beans, and lentils	Eat a variety of fruit Choose fresh, frozen, canned, or dried fruit Go easy on fruit juices	Go low-fat or fat-free when you choose milk, yogurt, and other milk products If you don't or can't consume milk, choose lactose-free products or other calcium sources such as fortified foods and beverages	Choose low-fat or lean meats and poultry Bake it, broil it, or grill it Vary your protein routine — choose more fish, beans, peas, nuts, and seeds

For a 2,000-calorie diet, you need the amounts below from each food group. To find the amounts that are right for you, go to MyPyramid.gov.

Eat 6 oz. every day	Eat 2 1/2 cups every day	Eat 2 cups every day	Get 3 cups every day; for kids aged 2 to 8, it's 2	Eat 5 1/2 oz. every day

Find your balance between food and physical activity
- Be sure to stay within your daily calorie needs.
- Be physically active for at least 30 minutes most days of the week.
- About 60 minutes a day of physical activity may be needed to prevent weight gain.
- For sustaining weight loss, at least 60 to 90 minutes a day of physical activity may be required.
- Children and teenagers should be physically active for 60 minutes every day, or most days.

Know the limits on fats, sugars, and salt (sodium)
- Make most of your fat sources from fish, nuts, and vegetable oils.
- Limit solid fats like butter, stick margarine, shortening, and lard, as well as foods that contain these.
- Check the Nutrition Facts label to keep saturated fats, *trans* fats, and sodium low.
- Choose food and beverages low in added sugars. Added sugars contribute calories with few, if any, nutrients.

physical activity (Stein, 1999). However, more recently, there are still a variety of diets that promote weight loss by different methods, and a balance must be found. The "low cal[orie]" diet has been called the "tried and true" approach and is the one most often recommended by mainstream nutritionists, with insights from other diets often assimilated in it. The low-cal diet simply says that "a calorie is a calorie is a calorie." One is bound to lose weight by making sure that fewer calories are eaten than the body burns. The results are better if you include an exercise program (Bjerklie et al., 2002). The bottom line is that the debate over diets will continue for a long time to come. You must find, preferably with your doctor's advice, the best eating plan for you to maintain your health and weight control. The choices of diets are up to you, but get the advice of a qualified nutritionist or a physician.

Watch Your Calories and Fats

Whenever diets are discussed, the "calorie" comes up. Simply defined, the energy in our food and the energy our bodies use are measured in calories. Calories are present in carbohydrates, proteins, and fats; there are no calories in fiber, water, vitamins, and minerals. Calories play a crucial role in weight maintenance. If you use more calories (in exercise and physical activities) than you take in through foods, you will lose weight; if you take in and use equal amounts of calories, your weight will stay the same; and if you take in more calories than you use, you will gain weight (Charlesworth and Nathan, 1984).

Diets high in saturated fat and cholesterol can lead to high blood-cholesterol levels—a contributing factor in heart disease. However, some fat in your diet is good for you because both carbohydrates and fats are sources of energy. Fat also help organs absorb, store, and transport some vitamins, as well as aid digestion. Although we need some fat in our diets, when we consume more fat than our bodies need, the excess is stored in our tissues, especially around our midsections. You constantly should be aware of the amount of fat you take in. Do not rule out fat altogether. Fats are essential for good health. Fats provide energy, essential hormone-like substances, and vital fatty acids for healthy skin. Fats also carry the fat-soluble vitamins A, D, E, and K, through the body while at the same time helping the body to absorb them (International Food Information Council Foundation, courtesy of Weight Watchers, Inc., 2004).

Watch Your Helpings

Stressed-out correctional workers often overeat. To control the intake of fat and calories, you should limit the number of servings you eat. For example, one serving from the breads, cereals, rice, and pasta group could mean one slice of bread or one ounce of ready-to-eat cereal. A half can of fruit (of the average size of eight ounces) is one serving from the fruit group. To control your weight, avoid having too many high-calorie or high-fat servings. Eat small servings and avoid "seconds."

Good nutrition is a science that can take years of training to fully understand. However, you now know enough to begin thinking about how you can improve your diet regimen.

Suggestions for Healthier Eating

1. Take a self-exam of your eating habits. Do you eat a balanced diet? Do you eat too much junk food? If so, plan to change.

2. Get educated. You can find books, pamphlets, and articles on healthy, low-fat eating in books, magazines, and at your local grocery, bookstore, or community medical center. Speak to the staff where you have your annual physical exam.

3. Cut down on the amount of beef, ham, and pork you eat. Eat fish, veal, and chicken without skin instead.

4. Chill soups and gravies after preparation, then skim off the congealed fat.

5. Cut down on fried foods, such as French fries and fried chicken. Broil or bake foods. If you must fry or sauté foods, use a nonstick frying pan or a vegetable-oil nonstick spray. Also, use oils such as canola that do not contain transfatty acids.

6. Cut down on salt. Use less or no salt to flavor foods. Many foods already have a lot of salt in them. Lowering your sodium intake helps lower your blood pressure.

7. Read labels. Find out how many calories, fat (especially transfat), cholesterol, and carbohydrates are in the foods you are eating. Watch your servings!

8. Trim off excess fats from meats and remove the skin from poultry before you cook.

9. Reduce your intake of refined sugars, such as baked goods, candy bars, and soda. Substitute honey for sugar. Fruits, grains, nuts, potatoes, and pasta produce complex carbohydrates, which produce the sugars your body needs.

10. Increase your consumption of fruits and vegetables. These produce fiber that helps your intestines function.

11. Eat whole grains (bran, whole wheat bread, and brown rice), beans and legumes that also contain fiber, which makes you feel full so you will not overeat.

12. Buy cookbooks containing healthy recipes.

13. Cut down on alcoholic beverages. They are high in calories (one twelve-ounce beer contains approximately 150 calories).

14. Drink a lot of water. Water has no calories, aids digestion, and helps flush impurities from your system. Spice it up with a slice of lime. Drink mineral water.

15. Fruit juices often are high in calories (for example, one eight-ounce glass of orange juice has approximately 110 calories). Dilute the calories by mixing the juice with club soda, mineral water, or seltzer.

16. Cut down on the number of meals per week you eat at fast food restaurants. Many items offered at fast food restaurants are high in fat and calories.

17. Ask family members to take turns cleaning up after a meal so you can get away from the kitchen. You will be less tempted to pick or nibble.

18. Slow down when you eat—chew slowly. Do not gobble down your food. Eating slowly will help you feel full. Wait twenty minutes before going back for seconds— twenty minutes is about how long it takes for your meal to trigger the sensation of being full.

19. If you crave "munchies" at night, eat low-fat, low-calorie snacks, such as raw vegetables or fruit.

20. Do not shop for food when you are hungry, because you will be inclined to purchase temptation foods.

21. Use imagery: See yourself thinner and refusing second helpings.

22. Food cravings usually will pass within twenty minutes. During that time, stay away from the kitchen. Never allow yourself to feel hungry.

23. Set eating times for meals and snacks and stick to them.

24. Eat pretzels instead of potato chips, they have less fat.

25. Eat air-popped popcorn instead of oil-popped popcorn. Try eating popcorn without butter and with little or no salt. For variety, you can add spices without salt.

26. Do not be at the mercy of a restaurant menu. Eat broiled instead of fried foods. Ask for plain baked potatoes without high-calorie toppings. Eat a lot of vegetables. Ask for sauces on the side and the skin removed from chicken. Look for low-fat items or items that are grilled. Get sauces and dressings on the side so you can control how much you eat.

27. Go to the restaurant salad bar and create your own low-fat meal. Avoid buffets. Substitute healthy foods for the not-so-healthy foods, such as a double helping of the vegetable of the day instead of mashed potatoes with the entrée. Most good eateries will let you. At a party, target the low-fat snacks.

28. Steam foods like vegetables, chicken, and fish without oils or butter.

29. Eat more salads, but skip noodles, croutons, and creamy dressings. Use lemon juice or reduced-calorie dressings.

30. Keep a food diary. Review daily what you ate, noting calorie and fat content. See if you made any mistakes and resolve to do better.

31. Plan your meals ahead of time. Write out a healthy menu for the next day and stick to it. Take your lunch to work—this can be both healthy and cheap.

32. Use skim or low-fat milk (if you do not like the taste of skim milk, some stores offer 1 percent or one-half percent milk).

33. Instead of regular ice cream, eat low-fat yogurt or ice milk.

34. Grilling meat on the barbecue or on a grill designed to drain cooking juices is beneficial. Calories are reduced and fats drip and sizzle away.

Nutrients Our Bodies Need

Stress depletes the body of many nutrients that are good for our nervous and glandular systems. As part of your education program on good nutrition, find out which foods contain essential vitamins and minerals. The following vitamins and minerals are recommended by the U.S. Department of Agriculture for good health (Pearson, 2000):

- vitamins A, C, D, E, and K
- B Group: thiamine (B1), riboflavin (B2), pyridoxine (B6), B12
- Folic acid
- Niacin
- Pantothenic acid (B5)
- Biotin
- Calcium
- Phosphorus
- Magnesium
- Iron
- Iodine
- Copper
- Zinc

35. If your workplace has a refrigerator and a microwave, keep a supply of frozen diet entrees and low-fat foods for lunches.

36. Do not skip meals. If you skip breakfast, you probably will overeat at lunch.

37. If planning a trip, pack a cooler with healthy foods instead of stopping at a fast-food restaurant.

38. Watch your coatings. Although chicken and fish are good for you, crispy coatings and breading add unnecessary calories.

39. Take advantage of modern science. If you like a particular food, look for it in a low-calorie or low-fat variety.

40. Substitute. Little things can do a lot. Look in your cookbooks for ways to substitute low-calorie foods for high-calorie ones. For example, when cooking or baking, substitute two egg whites for one whole egg. You will have less fat and cholesterol. When you bake, substitute low-calorie or "natural" applesauce for vegetable oil.

41. If you are exercising regularly, eat carbohydrate-laden foods, such as pasta, rice, and potatoes, a few hours before you exercise. This will help your endurance.

42. Be careful about egg yolks. Nutritionists recommended that people eat no more than two whole eggs per week due to eggs' high cholesterol content. However, egg whites do not have any cholesterol.

43. If you like cream in your coffee, try skim milk. It is better for you than nondairy creamers.

44. Avoid foods that leave fat stains on napkins or paper bags. They are loaded with grease you do not need.

45. Fresh fruits and vegetables should be crisp and firm. Freeze fresh vegetables before cooking to preserve nutrients, and do not soak produce in water because the nutrients will leak out.

46. Use polyunsaturated or mono-unsaturated oils, such as soybean, sunflower, cottonseed, canola, corn, olive, and safflower. Research indicates that in small amounts, these oils may help reduce cholesterol levels.

47. Eat more meatless meals. Try eating more salads, pasta, and bean and rice dishes.

48. Instead of butter or syrup on waffles and pancakes, try sugar-free jams or low-calorie syrup.

49. Before you eat, take a few deep breaths, relax, and sit down. Do not eat a meal standing up or on the run, such as while driving or walking.

50. Supplement your diet with vitamins to ensure you get all the vitamins you need. Take a multiple vitamin and mineral supplement.

51. Wherever possible, avoid eating commercially prepared foods containing animal fats, coconut oil, palm oil, and large amounts of sugar.

52. Cook with various spices to increase flavor. Be sure the spice does not contain added salt. Many of the combination spices have salt as the first ingredient.

53. Go grocery shopping with a set list and buy only the foods on that list. This also will save you money.

54. If it is necessary to prepare fatty, greasy, or salty foods, give the leftovers away. Do not take them home.

55. Remember: eat more complex carbohydrates and high fiber. Complex "carbs" are found in many whole grain foods, fresh fruits and vegetables. Fiber, sometimes called "roughage" is found in whole grains, vegetables, and fruits such as apples and citrus fruit. Both complex carbohydrates and fiber help you feel full (Cooper and Cooper, 1996).

56. Be careful when using artificial sweeteners. Some studies suggest that artificial sweeteners such as those found in diet foods have little or no effect on weight control and reduction of calories. Artificial sweeteners block the cues to the brain that we are full, and that is why you still may be hungry after having something that is artificially sweetened. It may be more beneficial to use moderate amounts of less-refined sugars (Cooper and Cooper, 1996).

57. Look at healthy eating as a lifestyle habit, not just going on a diet.

58. No dessert until the meal is finished. Then, you may be too full for dessert, and may settle for a low-sugar, low-fat snack later.

59. Like ice cream? Get a single and not a double dip. Get a dish and skip the cone. Get a skim milk malt or shake.

60. Have ONE helping and slowly enjoy every bite.

61. Have a craving for chocolate? Eat a small part of a brownie, or other delectable and walk away.

62. Learn to combine healthy eating and socializing. If coworkers go to a burger place for lunch, you can bring your prepared lunch. However, many of these places now offer salads or sandwiches with lettuce instead of bread.

63. At family gatherings when the favorite meal is served, eat a little of it and eat more of the vegetables and salads.

64. Never go to bed hungry.

65. While cooking, chew sugar-free gum.

66. Buy food in smaller quantities so you have less or no leftovers.

67. Use nighttime brushing your teeth as your signal that eating and snack time are over.

68. Going to a social gathering where a lot of food is going to be there? Eat before you go.

69. At a party or social event, concentrate on the other guests and conversation, not on the food and drink. Position yourself away from the buffets, snacks, and the bar.

70. Paste a photo of yourself where you see it everyday. If you are heavy in the photo, it will remind you to stay on track. If it is of you when you were slender, it will also remind you to stay on your plan.

See the following publications in the reference section of this book. The author recommends the following:

- Robert K. Cooper and Leslie L. Cooper, *Low Fat Living*
- Walter C. Willett. M.D., *Eat, Drink, and Be Healthy: The Harvard Medical School Guide to Healthy Eating,*
- Dr. Phil McGraw, *The Ultimate Weight Solution*

You can find other solutions by contacting such organizations such as Weight Watchers, Inc., or by consulting with a nutritionist or your family doctor.

Exercise Guide

If you have not exercised in a long time or have not had a physical exam recently, you should consult your doctor to discuss your physical fitness goals and ascertain any risks. Your physician may recommend an exercise stress test, such as a treadmill or stationary bicycle, during which your heart condition and blood pressure will be checked. Exercise tests are recommended for healthy people age forty-five or older or those older than thirty-five having at least one coronary risk factor (such as obesity) and people who are sedentary, smoke, have high blood pressure, and/or have heart disease in their family history. Also, people who are diabetic, have high cholesterol levels, or have abnormal readings in an electrocardiogram should be checked. Any type of heart or lung ailment dictates the necessity of an exercise test. A tell-tale "alarm" signal is chest pains occurring during any kind of physical activity. Play it safe and get checked out. Not only will you find out the status of your health, but you will have peace of mind as well (Powell, 1992).

Not every type of exercise appeals to everyone. The key is to find an exercise or activity that you like and stick with it. Swimming, for example, may be enjoyable for some, but not for others. Some may prefer fast walking over running. Exercise should be enjoyable and interesting.

One of your first steps is to set goals and determine which strategies will get you there. Ask yourself the following questions (Powell, 1992):

1. How fit am I? (Poor, fair, or good?)

2. What are my goals? Endurance, strength, or flexibility? All?

3. Can I stay with it? Is it feasible considering my home and work schedules?

4. How will I measure my progress? Weight checks? A physical exam in six months?

5. What exercises and activities will I do?

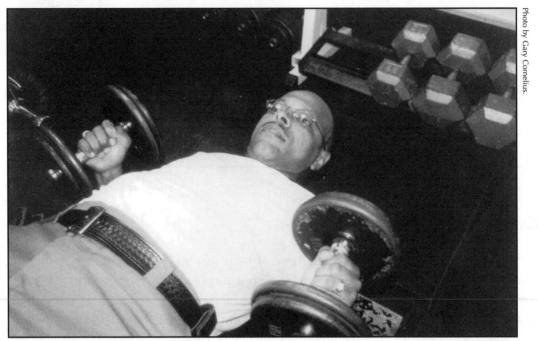

Photo by Gary Cornelius.

Getting exercise, a little or a lot, wherever and whenever you can, will help you feel better and reduce tension.

The best plans are written. You can make up a chart with the type of exercises and the number of times or repetitions you will perform them.

Once you get started, you must continue. Here are some guidelines:

1. Do not make excuses. For every excuse, there is a reason why you should exercise.

2. Do not give up if you do not see immediate results. It may take a few months (some research says three to six) to feel comfortable or to see significant weight loss.

3. Set short-term goals. Plan your activities week by week. For example, determine that this week you will swim three times, twenty laps per session. Maybe next week you will increase that goal.

Choosing Exercises

For correctional work, aerobic exercises that develop your heart and lung capacity, such as running, walking, swimming, jogging, bicycling, dancing, and stair climbing, are most beneficial. Isometric exercises, such as weight lifting and pushing against immovable objects (a wall), build muscular endurance and strength. Although exercise is stress, it is good stress. Your body is reacting to change, but due to the release of certain hormones, you get a psychological "high" from the activity. The good stress from exercise thus benefits you mentally as well as physically.

Do Not Let Your Excuses Win Out

Excuse: "I can't work out. It takes too much time."

Comeback: All that is necessary is twenty-to-thirty minutes, three-to-five days a week, or some type of daily activity.

Excuse: "I do not feel like it. I'm too tired."

Comeback: Exercise can recharge and reenergize.

Excuse: "I'm not an athlete."

Comeback: A stress-management exercise program does not require Olympic skills. One can swim, walk, or shoot baskets in a local park.

Excuse: "I get bored."

Comeback: Vary your routine with several activities; exercise with friends.

Excuse: "I'm too old."

Comeback: Exercise can begin at any age. It is never too late.

Excuse: "I can't afford it."

Comeback: Walking and running require proper shoes and space; activities such as swimming and tennis may require inexpensive equipment and small fees at recreation centers or parks.

In choosing an exercise, take advantage of the marketplace. There are many products available to help you—from exercise videos you can follow in your home to equipment, such as rowing machines, weight training equipment, and cross-country skiing machines. Many are portable and fold up. In many areas, local recreation centers offer inexpensive aerobics classes and have available swimming, weight training, tennis, and racquetball facilities. You may want to join a health club that has a wide range of equipment and classes.

The important thing is to get educated and exercise. Talk to weight trainers and fitness instructors about the proper way to do exercises. Do not jump in too fast. Start slowly and gradually and reduce the risk of injury. Most importantly: maintain a positive attitude and believe in yourself.

Calorie Burning

Not only can regular, planned exercise burn off calories, but you can incorporate calorie burning into everyday, routine activities. For example, at work, be mobile. If you are on a tier, walk around more instead of sitting. Sitting and taking a coffee break every ten minutes burns eighteen calories, while taking a stroll around the office for ten minutes burns thirty-five calories. Climbing stairs burns up more calories than riding an escalator or elevator.

At home, the same principle applies. During the summer, mowing the lawn or washing the car burns calories. For example, a 150-pound adult doing an hour of light housework uses 246 calories an hour. If the same adult scrubbed floors for an hour, he or she would burn up 440 calories. The chart on page 166 gives an overview of some basic exercise activities.

As you develop your exercise program, keep the following tips in mind:

1. Start slowly. Do not try to jog five miles your first day. If you are beginning aerobics, start with low-impact aerobics (one foot on the floor at all times). If lifting weights, work into it gradually. Start with someone who is knowledgeable, such as a trainer. Pace yourself.

2. Listen to qualified personnel. Consult with people who are knowledgeable about fitness and listen to them.

3. Be careful outside. Walk, run, or jog in safe areas and wear protective clothing. During strenuous activity, take breaks often.

4. Cover exposed skin and run among buildings that block chilling winds in cold weather.

5. Work out two to three hours after a meal and one to two hours after a snack.

6. Do not risk illness or injury due to excessive heat. If you exercise outdoors during the summer, do it in the early morning or after the sun goes down. Drink eight to ten ounces of water ten to fifteen minutes before you start. Have water handy to drink during your activity. Drink at least eight-to-ten eight ounce glasses per day.

7. Do not buy athletic shoes or outer wear without checking out information on them. Stores that exclusively handle athletic wear, including footgear, are everywhere. Trained staff will answer your questions and help you make the best choice.

8. Warm up and cool down. To avoid injury, workouts, including aerobics, should include five to ten minutes of warm ups before the main workout and five to ten minutes of cooling down afterwards. Many exercise programs, classes, and videos have these two phases built in.

9. Get plenty of rest and sleep; exercising is tougher when you are tired.

10. When beginning an exercise program, exercise weekly on three nonconsecutive days and as time goes on exercise on alternate days.

11. Try to exercise at the same time each day. This may not be possible all the time, so try to at least exercise according to a schedule. Do not exercise when you are extremely tired. Your alertness may be down and you may injure yourself or not do the exercises properly.

12. Follow good eating habits (*see* Appendix A).

13. Make exercise pleasant and convenient: For example, the pool is on your way home from work, the gym is clean and nearby. You may stop your program if you have to push yourself to get to a facility. Consider setting up a home gym or exercise space at home. Be cautious and set up a procedure for what to do in an emergency, such as an injury.

14. Combine social time and exercise time by exercising with friends.

15. Do "complete" physical activities, such as crossing over from swimming to aerobic dancing, tennis, rowing, weights, fast walking, calisthenics, and so forth This will condition and tone different parts of your body.

16. Reward yourself. When you reach a goal in your program, buy yourself something nice.

17. Replace negative thoughts with positive thoughts. When swimming lap number twenty, instead of thinking that "this is boring," think "I'm going to look so good when I have worked up to a mile twice per week."

18. Finish strenuous exercises gradually. If you do not, the effect of suddenly dropping your blood pressure and heart rate may make you dizzy or cramped. Wind down by doing light exercises after strenuous ones.

19. Breathe deeply and regularly.

20. Do not overstrain yourself. After exercising, take a five minute rest and count your pulse. If your pulse count is more than 120 beats per minute, you may be doing too much. Listen to the warning signs such as chronic fatigue, persistent aches and pains after exercising, loss of appetite, weight loss that cannot be explained, excessive thirst, sleep disturbances, serious hormonal changes, and severe gasping for breath during exercise. If these occur, see a doctor.

EXERCISE	BENEFITS	COST	CALORIES BURNED/HR	REMARKS
Aerobic dancing*	Heart/lungs	Low	Light 120 Moderate 200 Vigorous 300	Dancing, videos, exercise classes
Basketball	Heart/lungs	Low	450	Play with others
Bicycling	Heart/lungs, muscles	Moderate	174 at 5 MPH	Builds endurance
Circuit weight training	Muscle tone	Moderate to high	756	May have to purchase weights or join a club
Cycling* (stationary)	Heart/lungs/muscles	Moderate	5.5 MPH 130 10 MPH 220 13 MPH 320	Purchase equipment or join club
Dancing (ballroom)	Coordination, heart/lungs	Moderate	210	Social benefits
Golf (twosome, carrying clubs)	Heart/lungs coordination	Moderate	324	Outdoors social benefits
Horseback riding (sitting/trot)	Heart/lungs, coordination	Moderate to high	246	Outdoors
Jogging	Heart/lungs muscles	Low	10 minute mile at 6 MPH: 654	Use good running shoes
Racquet sports*	Overall conditioning	Low	Badminton: 175 Tennis: 210 Racquetball: 360 Squash: 420	Tennis courts are everywhere
Running*	Heart/lungs, lowers body fat	Low	5.5 MPH: 320 6 MPH: 350	Wear good shoes
Rowing*	Strengthens whole body	Low	Light: 200 Vigorous: 420	Variety of equipment on market
Swimming*	Overall conditioner, aerobic: heart/lungs	Low	25 yds/minute: 180 40 yds/minute: 260	May have to join club, depends on weather
Walking*	Aerobic, endurance Heart/lungs	Low	2.5 MPH: 105 4.5 MPH: 200 6 MPH: 370	Can do anytime and anywhere

(Hourly estimates based on calories burned for a 150 pound person. * Indicates calories burned for 150 pound person, add 10 percent for every fifteen pounds over this weight and subtract 10 percent for every fifteen pounds under this weight.)

(Powell, 1992; Van Itallie et al., 1987)

Appendix

Positive-Coping Methods

The following list of effective coping methods should give you some ideas about simple, everyday, inexpensive things you can do to manage stress. There is no set answer. The key is to be creative, a little unorthodox, and find stress-reducing methods that work for you. What is stress reducing for one may not be good for another. One thing to remember before you review this list: accept stress as a part of everyday life.

1. Read a good book. Read things that are *not* job related.
2. Go to a movie or rent a movie and have a "movie night."
3. Take a long, leisurely walk at least every other day.
4. Write a letter to a friend or family member.
5. Go window-shopping.
6. Take time off by leaving a half-day early (if possible). Take day trips, go on a vacation, or get away for a long weekend.
7. Go see a friend or neighbor.
8. Take a nap.
9. Telephone a friend or family member and "shoot the breeze."
10. Listen to your favorite music.
11. Clean out a closet or drawer and throw away junk.
12. Enjoy nature.
13. Attend a religious service.
14. Rearrange your house.
15. Go shopping and reward yourself with something.
16. Drive to a park and take a walk.

17. Take a fifteen-to twenty-minute "quiet" break every day.

18. Take a class or go back to school.

19. Quit smoking today.

20. Do not put things off.

21. Pick your friends carefully—have some friends who are not in the same field of work.

22. Say "no" more often and say "yes" less frequently.

23. Keep a sense of humor about yourself. Learn to laugh. You will feel better.

24. Be polite at all times.

25. Do not engage in gossip and rumors—you may lose friends.

26. Dress well and keep yourself clean.

27. Get enough sleep.

28. Compliment others and do not forget to compliment yourself once in a while.

29. No matter what the workload, take a "mental health" day off.

30. Do not live in the past, look to the future.

31. Delegate duties at work and at home.

32. Get a massage, or give a loved one a massage.

33. Take it easy and slow down.

34. Make a list of your successes.

35. Go out to dinner, lunch, or breakfast once in a while.

36. Face up to unpleasant situations.

37. Avoid excessive noise.

38. Avoid surprises.

39. Upon arriving home, put on loose-fitting clothes.

40. Enjoy your sexuality.

41. Begin an exercise program. Be active every day.

42. Watch what you eat.

43. Play with your children and/or pets.

44. Fix up your yard, garden, or home.

45. If you are being relied on, encourage others to take responsibility.

46. Give yourself credit.

47. Do something nice for yourself everyday.

48. Go sightseeing.

49. Change jobs, if necessary.

50. Learn to let go of things you cannot change. Avoid battles that are not worth fighting—they will wear you out.

51. Take up a hobby.

52. Host a party.

53. Buy a gift for a loved one for no special reason.

54. Look through an old photo album.

55. Soak in a hot bath.

56. Go to an amusement park.

57. For an energy boost, schedule a midday workout or brisk walk.

58. Create a cozy office or home environment with desk lamps, flowers, potted plants, and family pictures.

59. Take a few minutes and relive a happy memory or occurrence from the past.

60. Learn to do your best, and leave the rest.

61. Strive to unload excess [emotional] baggage that you have been carrying around.

62. Learn to back off, especially around those who tend to "push your buttons."

63. Be yourself. Do not try to appear as someone who you really are not.

64. Be aware of your limitations, especially before volunteering to do something,

65. Read books and articles requiring concentration—it is a good boost for your mind.

66. Live your life by the calendar—not by the stopwatch. Learn to manage time.

67. Cook a nice meal. Eat it slowly.

68. Practice visual imagery—imagine pleasant surroundings; it will calm you down.

69. Use modern technology, such as a computer, cell phone, fax machine, answering machine, and so forth to simplify your life.

70. Do isometric exercises—push one part of your body against another and tense for a few seconds. Do it for one minute. Tense and relax.

71. Get up and look out the window for one minute.

72. Stand up and stretch for one minute.

73. Start and end your day with meditation or a prayer.

74. Adopt a self-motto: "This work will be here the next day, so I will not take it home." "It is just a job; it is not my whole life." "The inmates will be here tomorrow, it can wait."

75. Talk to people, your family, your significant other, friends, and others about your stress.

76. Take an "alone break," where you get by yourself for a good length of time. Sort out what is stressing you out when you are away from a stressful situation.

77. Write down your thoughts and feelings in a private journal. Be honest, and do not hold back. This will allow you to look at your stressors and figure out what you can do about them in perspective.

78. If you are angry, punch a punching bag, beat a drum, or punch a pillow—*alone*.

79. Allow yourself to cry. It is okay.

80. Do not hold back or stuff stress into a corner, admit that it exists and it is a part of life.

Can you think of any others?

Relaxation Exercises

Many relaxation methods have been discussed in Chapter 8. The following scripts are examples of the calm scene, visual imagery, progressive muscle relaxation, and triggers of relaxation. You can obtain exercises such as these in many books currently on the market or you can check with your local mental health agency or EAP counselor about obtaining an audiotape cassette. You can memorize a script, but you may find it easier to read the instructions yourself into a tape recorder in a soft, calm voice. When you play the tape back, you can hear your own soothing voice as you follow the instructions.

Set the stage for your relaxation exercise by doing the following:

- Wear comfortable, loose-fitting clothes. Do not wear work clothes or uniforms if you are at home
- Clear the area of distractions and noise: no telephone, television, radio, or children
- Do not eat, drink, smoke, or chew gum during the exercise
- Choose a comfortable way to sit, lie down, or recline, such as on a comfortable chair, recliner, sofa, or floor mat
- Dim the lights

Calm Scene

Sit or lie down comfortably. It is time to relax. Slowly close your eyes. Take a deep, slow breath, count slowly to three, and then exhale out of your mouth. Do it two more times. Think, "I am relaxed." "I am calm."

Imagine yourself in a place where you feel peaceful, calm, and relaxed. You are lying on the beach on a warm, sunny day. You can see the waves lapping up on the sand in a steady rhythm. You feel the warm sea air flowing over you in a soft breeze. You can feel the heat of the sand between your toes. Breathe deeply and savor the feelings of relaxation and warmth. You think of the fresh sea smell and hear the seagulls flying overhead. You can see yourself lying there feeling the warmth of the sun on your body, listening to the steady beat of waves.

Relax. Think of how relaxed and calm you are feeling. [Pause for 10 seconds]

Just relax and think of the beach for a little while. [Long pause for 45 seconds]

Now, slowly open your eyes. Take another deep breath. Slowly get up and realize how relaxed and less tense you feel. Take as long as you want before you resume your day.

[End of Calm Scene]

This example involved a beach scene, but you can set the scene in the woods, a meadow, or any other scene you find soothing and peaceful.

Visual Imagery

Similar to the calm scene, this method involves focusing your mind on pleasant thoughts and images and creating a picture in your mind. Sit comfortably, close your eyes, breathe deeply, and think of an image that is relaxing to you. Try it for five, ten, or twenty minutes.

Progressive Relaxation

Progressive relaxation means alternately tensing and relaxing major muscle groups of your body. Think of the major regions of your body: head and neck, shoulders, arms and hands, chest, abdomen, legs, and feet. Each region will be relaxed. Do not do this within two hours after a meal due to the fact that digestion may interrupt the process. You can follow a script for progressive relaxation the same way as in the calm-scene exercise. Relax for ten seconds after you tighten a muscle.

Caution: During tensing or tightening, do not hold your breath. Do not tighten or tense any part of your body that is weak or injured.

Sit comfortably in a chair. Your forearms should rest, palms downward, on the arms of the chair or on your lap. Relax. Take a deep, slow breath, count slowly to three, and then exhale out of your mouth. Do it two more times.

You are going to relax by doing a few simple things. You are going to first tighten each muscle, then relax and let the tensions flow away. [Pause for five seconds]

Start with your face. Frown as hard as you can for ten seconds. Frown . . . slowly count to ten . . . relax. Squeeze your eyes shut tightly. Slowly count to ten . . . relax. Now, take your nose. Wrinkle it for ten seconds . . . relax. Press your lips together tightly . . . tightly . . . tightly . . . count to ten . . . relax. [Pause for 5 seconds]

And now . . . your neck. Tuck your chin against your chest tightly . . . count slowly to ten . . . relax. Do it again. [Pause for 5 seconds]

Press your back hard against the chair . . . count to ten . . . relax . . . repeat. [Pause for 10 seconds]

Now, loosen up your shoulders and arms. You should feel the tension starting to melt away. You feel warmth flowing through your body. [Pause for 5 seconds]

Take your left shoulder and bring it up in a tight shrug . . . relax . . . repeat . . . do the same thing with the right shoulder. [Pause for 5 seconds]

And now your arms and hands. Bend each arm at the elbows and wrists. With each hand make a fist. Clench each fist tightly for ten seconds . . . tightly . . . relax. [Pause for 10 seconds]

Tighten your stomach muscles. Count slowly to ten . . . tighten . . . relax. Continue to breathe . . . slowly . . . deeply. [Pause for 10 seconds]

Now . . . your legs. Lift up your legs. Extend them, stretch them out. Count to ten . . . stretch them tightly . . . relax. [Pause for 10 seconds]

Flex your feet by stretching your toes back toward you as much as you can. Flex them tightly . . . tightly . . . tightly . . . count to ten . . . relax. Feel the tension flow out through your toes . . . repeat.

Concentrate on how warm, calm, and relaxed you feel. Feel the warm energy. Let yourself go limp. Allow your head, shoulders, and arms to drop forward.

Take a few minutes for yourself. When you are ready, open your eyes. You are refreshed . . . Resume your day.

(End of Progressive Relaxation exercise)

One final word of advice: If you find yourself thinking distracting thoughts, try to ignore them. Focus on your breathing and the goal of relaxation.

Triggers of Relaxation: When confronted with a stressor at home (such as loud children, a pile of bills, and so forth or a stressor at work, such as being called to the captain's office or a problem inmate requesting to see you, many of us feel the alarm stage and "awfulize"— imagining that things are worse than they are. To reduce the physical and mental wear and tear on ourselves, we must learn to turn on the relaxation button quickly. Here are several triggers that can be used to relax on the spot:

Code Words

Words or slogans that can be used to defuse or calm down when faced with stressors:

- "Calm down"
- "I can handle this".
- "I will be going home today."
- "Slow down"
- "Oh, well"

Come up with your own words, and remember to breathe deeply.

Deep Breathing

When confronted with the stressor, take a few moments to breathe deeply, in and out, in and out. Doing this is better than reacting angrily, snapping at those around us, or getting visibly upset. Simply follow these steps:

First: Sit up straight. Inhale from the bottom of your stomach below where the diaphragm begins. Allow your stomach to swell out as you slowly pull in the air. Inhale slowly and envision the air coming from the bottom of your lungs near the waist to the top near your shoulders. Let your chest swell out.

Second: If you feel tension in a particular part of your body, think about channeling the air to that part.

Third: Hold the air for a moment, and then breathe it out as slowly as you breathed it in. Slowly, push it out with your stomach muscles, which will pull in. Repeat over and over until you are breathing comfortably.

While doing so, say or think to yourself:

"Calm down." "I am relaxed."

Practice this until it becomes a natural part of your stress-management routine.

Source: Whittlesey, 1986.

Countdown

While breathing deeply, count down slowly from ten to one. Some people count from one to ten.

Relaxing Activities

These can include listening to soft music or pleasing sounds, soaking in a tub or napping.

Sample Charts

Often, stress-management methods can be clearer and easier to follow if we simply write them down. The same is true for time management. Writing a To Do list provides us with a plan we can follow to get things done without stress. This section contains an example of a stress-management goal plan or chart and a sample To Do list. You can use these, modify them, or get some ideas of your own.

Personal Stress Management Plan

My goals are

1. _____

_____

_____

2. _____

_____

_____

My activities (stress-management strategies) for goal number:	Start date for activity
_____	_____
_____	_____
_____	_____
_____	_____
_____	_____
_____	_____
_____	_____
_____	_____
_____	_____
_____	_____
_____	_____

Personal Stress-Management Plan for:

_____

My stressors are the following:

The physical and/or mental effects of my stressors are as follows:

1.

1.

2.

2.

3.

3.

4.

4.

5.

5.

6.

6.

7.

7.

8.

8.

To Do List

Week of: _____ Page: _____

Date	Task/Priority	Due Date	Delegate	Remarks

Notes/Reminders:

Follow Up:

Planning Ahead:

Appendix

This was the questionnaire used to generate the results shown in the text.

QUESTIONNAIRE

Stressed Out! 2nd Edition
Due October 21, 2002
To: Alice Fins, ACA, 4380 Forbes Boulevard, Lanham, MD 20706

Background

1. Name (optional): _____

2. Facility/Agency: _____

3. Sex: Male _____ Female _____ Age _____ Years in Corrections _____

4. Marital status:
_____ Married _____ Single _____ Divorced _____ Separated

5. Children: _____ yes _____ no
   If yes: number and ages: _____

6. Is your spouse also employed in corrections? Yes _____ No _____

7. What is your specific job title? What are your responsibilities?
   Circle the responsibilities that cause you the most stress.

   _____

   _____

   _____

8. Are you a supervisor? Yes _____ No _____

9. Area of corrections: Probation/Parole _____ Juvenile _____
   Community Corrections _____ Adult Local (jail) _____
   Prison _____ Other *(please specify):* _____

10. Civilian _____ Sworn _____

11. Shift Work? Yes _____ No _____

12. Does your job involve daily contact with inmates/offenders?
    Yes _____ No _____

13. Briefly describe contact (work housing areas, classification, etc.)

    _____

    _____

    _____

<u>Stress</u>

14. Rate your stress level:
    on duty: _____ high _____ medium _____ low
    off duty: _____ high _____ medium _____ low

15. Check any or all of the symptoms that stress causes you to have:

_____ Poor concentration	_____ Headaches
_____ Short term memory loss	_____ Muscle spasms
_____ Accident proneness	_____ Cold hands/feet
_____ Smoking	_____ Back & neck pain
_____ Overeating	_____ Ulcers
_____ Under eating	_____ "Sick feeling"/ nausea
_____ Decreased work output	_____ Diarrhea/constipation
_____ Overreacting to minor problems	_____ Rapid pulse
_____ Anger	_____ Shortness of breath
_____ Impatience	_____ Teeth grinding
_____ Anxiety	_____ Skin problems
_____ Increased use of drugs	_____ Sexual problems
_____ Increased use of alcohol	_____ Colds/flu
_____ Increased us of caffeine	_____ Increased perspiration
_____ Boredom	_____ Sleep difficulties
_____ Disruptions in work situations	_____ Fatigue/low energy
_____ Cannot release tension	_____ Abnormal heart rhythm
_____ Cannot relax	_____ Upset stomach
_____ Difficulty making decisions	_____ Weakness/ dizziness

Other(s): _____

16. What things in your life at work and at home cause stress (stressors)? Check all that apply:

____ Low salary	____ Lack of promotional opportunities
____ Tight deadlines	____ Boredom
____ Shift work	____ High staff turnover
____ Short staffing	____ Large caseloads
____ Inmate/offender demands	____ Bureaucratic red tape/ paperwork
____ Inmate arguments	____ Cramped working conditions
____ Argumentative families & attorneys	____ Excessive noise & bad odors
____ Court appearances	____ Exposure to body fluids & feces
____ Internal affairs investigations	____ Offender lies & manipulation
____ Substandard buildings/ equipment	____ Emergencies: fires, etc.
____ No clear guidelines or written procedures	____ On the job injuries
____ Conflicting decisions from supervisors	____ Pre-sentence report guidelines
____ Conflicting operations among shifts	____ Aggressive/violent offenders
____ Lack of support from supervisors	____ Offenders with mental disorders
____ No recognition for good work	____ Being sued or target of grievance
____ Lack of input in decision making	____ Escapes
____ Inadequate training	____ Lack of time
____ Poor communication	____ Bills

____ Feelings of failure: offenders /inmates not responding to your efforts

____ Offenders under influence of drugs & alcohol

____ Home/family responsibilities

____ Traffic/commuting

____ Lazy colleagues

____ Relatives

Other (s): _____

17. What stress management techniques do you use to cope with stress in your life?

____ Exercise	____ Taking leave	____ Proper diet
____ Hobby	____ Family activities	____ Talking to supervisor
____ Relaxation	____ Training	____ Visual imagery
____ Religion	____ Job reassignment	____ Progressive relaxation
____ Seeing a counselor	____ Talking to family	____ Talking to friends
____ Time management		

Other (s): _____

18. As a corrections professional, what would you like to see a book on handling correctional stress include or explore?

_____

_____

_____

19. Comments: Please add any other information that you think may be useful to reduce stress for those in corrections. Add other pages, if needed.

_____

_____

_____

_____

_____

Thank you for taking the time and effort to complete this survey. Please note that some questions require multiple responses. If you have any comments or would like additional information, or more questionnaires for colleagues, please contact ACA. Please return the questionnaires in the enclosed envelopes to ACA, 4380 Forbes Blvd., Lanham, MD 20706 by October 21, 2002.

Bibliography and Suggested Reading

Adler, Jerry, Claudia Kalb, and Adam Rogers. 1999. Stress. *Newsweek*. June 1, pp. 56ff.

Albrecht, Steve. 1999. Keeping it All in Balance. In Peter Pranzo and Rachela Pranzo, eds. *Stress Management for Law Enforcement*. Gould Publications, Longwood, Florida.

———. 1999. Running Out of Gas: Police Officers and Compassion Fatigue. In Peter Pranzo and Rachela Pranzo, eds. *Stress Management for Law Enforcement*. Gould Publications, Longwood, Florida.

Allen, Harry E., Clifford E. Simonsen, and Edward J. Latessa. 2004. *Corrections in America: An Introduction, 10th ed.* Upper Saddle River, New Jersey: Prentice Hall.

American Correctional Association. 1986. *Correctional Supervisors Correspondence Course, Book I: Basic Concepts in Supervision*. Lanham, Maryland: American Correctional Association.

———. 1986. *Correctional Supervisors Correspondence Course. Book II. Advanced Concepts in Supervision*. Lanham, Maryland: American Correctional Association.

———. 2003. Wages and Benefits Paid to Correctional Employees. *Corrections Compendium*. 28, 1. January.

———. 2003a. Correctional Officers and Drug Abuse. *Corrections Compendium*. 28 (4). April.

———. 2004. *2004 Directory of Juvenile and Adult Correctional Departments and Institutions, Agencies, and Probation and Parole Authorities*. Lanham, Maryland: American Correctional Association.

American Heart Association. What Do Your Cholesterol Numbers Mean? November 6, 2004. http://www.s2mw.com/cholesterollowdown/numbers.html http://www.s2mw.com/cholesterollow down/affects.html

American Institute of Stress. 2004. Job Stress. www.stress.org/job.htm

American Lung Association. 2004. www.American Lung Association.com

Ayres, R. and G. Flanagan. 1990. *Preventing Law Enforcement Stress: The Organization's Role*. Washington, D.C.: Bureau of Justice Assistance.

Barley, B. G. 1987. Stress and Disease. *Ladies' Home Journal*. May: 132-134.

Barnhart, C. and R. K. Barnhart. 1979. *The World Book Dictionary, Vol. 1*. Chicago: Doubleday/World Book.

Bartollas, Clemens. 2004. *Becoming a Model Warden: Striving for Excellence*. Lanham, Maryland: American Correctional Association.

Benson, H. et al. 1987. *Managing Stress from Morning to Night*. Alexandria, Virginia.: Time-Life Books.

Bjerklie, David with Sora Song, Dan Cray, and Elizabeth Kauffman. 2002. Cracking the Fat Riddle. *Time*, September 2, pp. 45 ff.

Brehm, Barbara A. 2002. Should You Make Time to Exercise? *Fitness Management.*

Bren, Linda. 2002. Losing Weight: More than Counting Calories. FDA/Office of Public Affairs, *FDA Consumer Magazine*, January-February.

Brown, D. 1990. Caseload, Turnover Problems Overwhelm Probation Officers. *Washington Post*. February 24, B1, 5.

Cabaniss, V., L. Harvey, and G. Kennedy. 1985. Sharing Career Perspectives: Four Stories from the Line (a Compilation). *Corrections Today*. 47(4): 12, 16.

Camp, Camille Graham. 2003. *The Corrections Yearbook: Adult Corrections 2002*. Middletown, Connecticut: Criminal Justice Institute, Inc.

Camp, Camille Graham and George M. Camp. 1999. *The Corrections Yearbook 1999*. Middletown, Connecticut: Criminal Justice Institute, Inc.

Campbell, K. 1985. Sharing Career Perspectives: Four Stories from the Line (a compilation). *Corrections Today*. Vol. 47, No. 4, July p.14.

Carr, John. 2003. Personal Communication.

Carter, D. 1992. The Status of Education and Training in Corrections. *Journal of Correctional Training*. (Winter): 6-9.

Champion, D. 1990. *Corrections in the United States: A Contemporary Perspective*. Englewood Cliffs, New Jersey: Prentice Hall.

Champion, Dean J. 2002. *Probation, Parole and Community Corrections, 4th ed.* Upper Saddle River, New Jersey: Prentice Hall.

Charlesworth, E. and R. G. Nathan. 1984. *Stress Management: A Comprehensive Guide to Wellness*. New York: Ballatine Books.

Cheek, F. E. 1983. Stress: How Not To Bring It Home. *Corrections Today*. Vol. 45, No. 1, February, pp. 14.

————. 1984. *Stress Management for Correctional Officers and Their Families*. Lanham, Maryland: American Correctional Association.

Consumer Information Center: The Food Guide Pyramid. www.pueblo.gsa.gov/cic_text/food/food-pryamid/main.htm

Cooper, Robert K. and Leslie L. Cooper. 1996. *Low Fat Living*. Emmaus: Rodale Press.

Cornelius, G. 1991. *Managing Stress Lesson Plan*. Lanham, Maryland: American Correctional Association.

————. 2001. *The Art of the Con: Avoiding Offender Manipulation*. Lanham, Maryland: American Correctional Association.

Correctional Officer Stress Management and Critical Incident Stress Management Program Material: NIJ/CLEFS Grant #2001-LT-BX-Ko13. Albert C. Wagner Youth Correctional Facility, New Jersey Department of Corrections. Program Manager: William Hepner.

Covey, Stephen and Hyrum Smith. 1999. What If You Could Chop an Hour from Your Day for the Things that Matter Most? *USA Weekend*. January 22, pp. 4-5.

Cox, Deborah. 2001. Anger: Express Yourself: Learn How to Express Your Anger Instead of Diverting It. abcnews.com

Cullen, Murray. 1992. *Cage Your Rage: An Inmate's Guide to Anger Control*. Lanham, Maryland: American Correctional Association.

Davis, Michael. 1995. Critical Incident Stress Debriefing: The Case for Corrections. *The Journal*. 2 (1): 58-59.

DeBruyn, H. C. 1989. Get Involved, Management By Walking Around Works. *Corrections Today*. Vol. 51, No. 5, August, p. 196.

DeWitt, Karen. 2003. Turn Chaos Into Calm: Interview with Dr. Andrea Sullivan. *Essence*. January: 99-102.

Engeler, A. 1993. When Silence Makes Sense. *Health*. 7, Jan.-Feb.: 94-97.

Escott International. 1987. *Stress Control: Create An Inner Calm by Bright Images*. BFS Limited, Richmond Hill, Ontario, Canada. Videocassette.

Evans, S. 1993. Driven Daily: They're Snoozing on a Sunday Afternoon. *Washington Post*. August 22.

Federal Citizen Information Center, www.pueblo.gsa.gov/results.tpl?id=1= 15&startat=1&—woSECTIONSdatarq=15&—S

Findlay, S. 1988. Mix and Match. *U.S. News and World Report*. July 18: 50-51.

Findlay, S., and T. Shryer. 1988. Smart Ways to Shape Up. *U.S. News and World Report*. July 18: 46-49.

Finn, Peter. 2000. *Addressing Correctional Officer Stress: Programs and Strategies*. NCJ 183474. Washington, D.C.: The National Institute of Justice.

Foa, Edna, R. T. Jonathan , Allen Davidson, Allen Frances, and Ruth Ross. *Expert Consensus Treatment Guidelines for Posttraumatic Stress Disorder: A Guide for Patients and Families.* Originally appearing in *Journal of Clinical Psychiatry,* 1999-60 (supplement 16). Obtained from Internet Mental Health (www.mental health.com).

Freudenburger, H. 1974. Staff Burnout. *Journal of Social Issues.* 30: 159-65.

———. 1980. *Burnout: The High Cost of High Achievement.* Garden City, New York: Anchor Press.

Fulton, Roger V. 1993. Commander, You Got a Minute? *Law Enforcement Technology.* July: 18.

Gaseau, Michelle. Before the Breaking Point: Solutions for Correctional Officer Stress. Corrections Connection, 08/04/03. www.corrections.com

Giant Food, Inc. 1993. *Eat for Health Food Guide.* Landover, Maryland.

Glock, A. 1993. *Anger: How to Handle It. Special Report.* Family Home Library. Vol. 2, No. 4. Knoxville, Tennessee: Whittle Communications.

Golin, M. 1988. New Age Prescriptions for Sound Health. *Prevention.* 40: 66-67, 112.

Grandjean, A. et al. 1987. *Eating Right: Recipes for Health.* Alexandria, Virginia: Time-Life Books.

Hales, Diane. 2001. Why Are We So Angry? *Parade.* September 2: 10-11.

Harper, S. 1992. *40 Ways to Beat Stress. Special Report.* Family Home Library. Vol. 1, No. 5. Knoxville, Tennessee: Whittle Communications.

Heim, T. 1991. A Case for the Case Study in Correctional Training. *Journal of Correctional Training.* Fall: 12-15.

Hellmich, N. 1993. For Moderate Exercises, New Guideline Reduces Guilt. *USA Today.* August 5: 4D.

Hellmich, Nanci. 2003. Fifth of Americans Report Exercise in Daily Routines. *USA Today.* May 15.

Hill, John. 2001. Corrections Deficit Near $200 Million. *Sacramento Bee.* Capitol Bureau. November 28. California State Employees Association News.

Hill, P. 1991. Job Burnout among Monmouth County Probation Officers—An Exploratory Study. San Jose, California: San Jose State University.

Honold, J. and J. Stinchcomb. 1985. Officer Stress: Costs, Causes and Cures. *Corrections Today.* Vol. 47, No. 7, December, pp. 46-51.

Hunt, N. J. 1994. Changes to Your Body When You Quit Smoking. *Capital Care Digest.* Winter: 11.

International Food Information Council Foundation: The Benefits of Balance: Managing Fat in Your Diet. Weight Watchers, Inc., Washington, D.C. www.ific.org

Johnson, E. H. 1992. Preliminary Survey of Personnel in American State Prison Systems. *Journal of Correctional Training.* Summer: 7-11.

Johnson, R. 1987. *Hard Time: Understanding and Reforming the Prison*. Monterey, California: Brooks-Cole.

Kauffman, K. 1988. *Prison Officers and their World*. Cambridge. Massachusetts: Harvard University Press.

Kennedy, Paula. 2003. The Top Five Diet Blunders. www.Weightwatchers.com, http://fitness.msn.com/articles/feeds/?dept=lose&article=lw_040903_dietblunders

Kiffer, Jerome F. 2002. Physical Warning Signs. The Cleveland Clinic. Web MD with AOL Health. Http://aolsvc.health.webmd.aol.com/content/pages/7/1674_ 52146?z=1674_52148_5003_0

Koopman, Marlene. 2003. National Institute of Justice Final Report: Southeast Iowa Correctional Family Program. December.

Koslow, Sally and Nancy Clark, NYT Women's Magazines. 1994. Family Circle's 500 Weight-loss Secrets. *Family Circle Magazine*, January: 19.

Lakein, A. 1973. *How to Get Control of Your Time and Your Life*. New York: Signet.

Lardner, James. 1999. World Class Workaholics. *U.S. News and World Report*. December 20: pp. 42ff.

Lemonick, Michael D. 2004. How We Grew So Big. *Time*. June 7: pp.57ff.

Lombardo, L. 1987. *Guards Imprisoned: Correctional Officers at Work, 2nd ed*. Cincinnati: Anderson.

Long, Philip. W. 1995-2003: Postraumatic Stress Disorder: American Description. Internet Mental Health (www.mentalhealth.com).

Lovrich, N. et al. 1990. *Staff Turnover and Stress in "New Generation" Jails: Key Implementation Issues for a Significant Correctional Policy*. Grant 89 JOIGH E3. Washington, D.C.: National Institute of Corrections.

Mackensie, R. A. 1985. Excerpts from the "Time Trap" handout. Virginia Department of Corrections.

Maltagliati, T. 1987. Risky Business. *Fairfax Journal*. December 8: B1-2.

Maltin, Lisa Jane. 2001. Religious, Spiritual Practices Good for Your Health: Reciting Ave Maria, Yoga Mantras Soothe Both Body and Soul. WebMD Corporation. http//:content.health.msn.com/printing/article 1689.51814

Manry, Kaitlin. 2003. What It's Like to Be "On Guard." *The Daily World*. April 3.

Mayo Clinic. Laughter and Medicine: How Humor Can Help You Heal. MayoClinic.com, www.mayoclinic.com 09/28/01, Mayo Foundation for Medical Education and Research (MFMER).

McCampbell, S. 1990. Direct Supervision: Looking for the Right People. *American Jails*. November-December: 68-69.

McCarthy, J. K. 1990. A Guide for Correctional Supervisors in Dealing with the Troubled Employee. In *1989 State of Corrections*. Lanham, Maryland: American Correctional Association.

McConkie, M. 1976. *Time Management in the Correctional Setting*. Athens, Georgia: University of Georgia.

McGraw, Philip C. 2003. *The Ultimate Weight Loss Solution: The 7 Keys to Weight Loss Freedom*. New York: The Free Press.

McQuade, W. and A. Aikman. 1974. *Stress*. New York: Bantam.

Meade, J. 1992. Take Control. *Men's Health*. 7: 38-42, 87.

Miller, A. et al. 1988. Stress on the Job. *Newsweek*. 11, April 25: 40-45.

Miller, L., A. Smith, and L. Rothstein. 1993. 21 Ways to Cope with Stress. *Ladies' Home Journal*. 110, April: 80-87.

Milloy, C. 1984. A Parole Officer with Toughest Cases in Town. *Washington Post*. May 11, C1, C4.

Monta, Howard A. 2002. *Survive Low Morale, Stress, and Burnout in Law Enforcement*. Longwood, Florida: Gould Publications.

Moore-Ede, M. 1983. *Shiftwork and Your Health*. Wellesley Hills, Massachusetts: Shiftwork Education Project.

Morris, R. 1986. Burnout: Avoiding the Consequences of On the Job Stress. *Corrections Today*. Vol. 48, No. 6, October, pp. 122ff.

Moynahan, J. M. 1999. Jail Officer Stress: There Is a Choice. *American Jails*. September-October: 71-78.

Natalucci-Persichetti, G. and A. P. Franklin. 1992. Managing a Changing Work Force. In *1991 State of Corrections*. Lanham, Maryland: American Correctional Association.

National Association of Chiefs of Police. 1995. *Chief of Police Medical Alert: Heed the Warnings: Stress Can Destroy Your Life*. January-February: 57.

National Institute on Alcohol Abuse and Alcoholism. 2004. News Release, June. www.NIAAA.nih. gov/press/2004.

National Institute of Justice, Corrections and Law Enforcement Family Support Program, www.ojp.usdoj.gov/nij/clefs/welcome.html

New Mexico Corrections Department CD-031300, Critical Incident Stress Debriefing. 02/26/94, Jim Burleson Interim Cabinet Secretary, NMCD.

Office of Juvenile Justice and Delinquency Prevention, Estimated Number of Juvenile Arrests, 2000. http://ojjdp.ncjrs.org/ojstatbb/html/qa250.html

O'Neill, Jack. 1993. *Stress Busters: 21 Thoughts for Your Emotional Wellness*. West Hartford: Derrymore West.

Oregon State Code: Title 18, Chapter 181. Statute: 181.860. 2001. West.

Parvin, J. 1993. How to Beat the Daily Grind. *Reader's Diges*t. 143, December: 185-190.

Pearson, James. 2000. *More than Muscle: A Total Fitness Program for Corrections and Law Enforcement*. Lanham, Maryland: American Correctional Association.

Pennsylvania Department of Corrections. *Minimize Your Stress, Maximize Yourself*. From Pennsylvania Department of Corrections Employees. Publication DC 556. Pennsylvania Department of Corrections.

Perdue, W. 1983. Seminar on criminal behavior, presented by the Virginia Department of Corrections. Fairfax, Virginia. December.

Perlmutter, C. 1991. Take a Moment to Muse. *Prevention*. 43, June: 38-41, 121.

Peterson, Karen. 2000. Why Is Everyone So Short Tempered? *USA Today*. July 18: 01A.

Pfeiffer, George J. and Judith Webster. 1992. *Workcare: A Resource Guide for the Working Person*. Charlottesville, Virginia: Workcare Press.

Phillips, Richard L. and Charles R. McConnell. 1996. *The Effective Corrections Manager: Maximizing Staff Performance in Demanding Times*. Gaithersburg, Maryland: Aspen Publishers.

Poe, R. 1987. Paying the Bill for Job Stress. *Washington Post*. February 20: 5.

Powell, D. 1992. *A Year of Health Hints*. Richmond: Health Management Corporation (Series 2 and 3).

Pranzo, Peter J. and Rachuela Pranzo. 1999. *Stress Management for Law Enforcement: Behind the Shield: Combatting Trauma*. Longwood, Florida: Gould Publications.

Psychiatric Institute of Washington, D.C. 1985. *Recognizing and Managing Stress*. Washington, D.C.: Psychiatric Institute of Washington, D.C.

Reese, J. 1987. Bureaucratic Burnout: A Challenge for Managers. *Behavioral Science in Law Enforcement*.

Rensberger, A. M. and M. E. Shine. 1989. Your Staff's Not Burned, It's Battered! In *1988 State of Corrections*. Lanham, Maryland: American Correctional Association.

Rhode Island Centurion Program. 2003. Brochure, John J. Carr, DCSW, Director.

Rich, S. 1993. Cigarette-related Deaths Decline. *Washington Post*. August 27: A4.

Rubin, Manning. 1993. *60 Ways to Relieve Stress in 60 Seconds*. New York: Workman Publishing.

Sacra, C. 1993. How to Turn Your Anger into Energy. *McCalls*. August: 86-9.

Sagon, Candy. 2001. Restaurant Rage. *Washington Post*. September 2: F1, F6.

Schaeffer, J. 1993. 20 *Ways to Gain More Personal Time. Special Report*. Family Home Library. Vol. 2, No. 6. Knoxville, Tennessee: Whittle Communications.

Schmidt, Barbara. 2004. Mark Twain Quotations, Newspaper Collections, and Related Resources. www.twainquotes.com

Schwiesow, D. and M. Bauman. 1994. Diet's Price Tag. *USA Today*. January 20: 1A.

Seiter, Richard P. 2002. *Correctional Administration: Integrating Theory and Practice*. Upper Saddle River, New Jersey: Prentice Hall.

Selye, H. 1974. *Stress without Distress*. New York: Signet.

Sharp, David. 1996. So Many Lists, So Little Time. *USA Weekend*. March 15-17: 4-6.

Slaby, A. 1988. *Sixty Ways to Make Stress Work for You*. Washington, D.C.: Psychiatric Institute of Washington, D.C.

Slon, S., ed. 1993. *101 Men's Health Secrets*. Emmaus, Pennsylvania.: Rodale Press.

Spake, A. 1985. Struggles in Stress City. *Washington Post Magazine*. January 13: 4-7, 16.

Squires, S. 1987. Are Americans Changing their Diets? *Washington Post*. October 6: Health Sciences Section, p. 6.

———. 2001. National Plan Urged to Combat Obesity. *Washington Pos*t. December 14, A3.

———. 2002. Experts Declare Story Low on Saturated Fats. *Washington Post*. August 27, HE01.

Stein, Joel. 1999. The Low-Carb Diet Craze. *Time*. November 1: 72-80.

———. 2004. The Low Fat Diet Craze. *Time*. November 1: 72-80.

Stoppler, Melissa C. 2004. Stress Management: Cortisol & Depression. About, Inc. http://stress.about.com/cs/cortisol/a/aa122803.htm.

Sugarman, C. 1993. Snacking on the Run. *Washington Post*. August 10: Health Sciences Section p. 16.

Take a Deep Breath. January 1994. *New Woman*.

Terhune-Bickler, Sandra D. 2004. Too Close for Comfort: Negotiating with Fellow Officers. *FBI Law Enforcement Bulletin*. 73(4): 1. April.

Thacker, J. 1990. Stress Management for Trainers—class presented at regional meetings, American Association of Correctional Training Personnel. Montgomery County, Maryland. December 13.

Thomas, N. M. 1990. The Impending Crisis: Expanding Demand, Shrinking Resources. In *1989 State of Corrections*. Lanham, Maryland: American Correctional Association.

Trautman, Neal. 2002. *How to be a Great Cop*. Upper Saddle River, New Jersey: Prentice Hall.

Ubell, E. 1990. The Deadly Emotions. *Parade Magazine*. February 11: 4-6.

Urquhart, Judith and Murray Cullen. 2003. *Cage Your Rage for Women*. Lanham, Maryland: American Correctional Association.

Van Itallie, T. et al. 1987. *Setting your Weight: A Complete Program*. Alexandria, Virginia: Time-Life Books.

Veninga, R. and J. Spradley. 1981. *The Work Stress Connection: How to Cope with Job Burnout*. New York: Ballantine Books.

Verdeyen, V. 1992. Wellness: An Important Lifestyle Choice for Correctional Officers. In *The Effective Correctional Officer*. Lanham, Maryland: American Correctional Association.

Walker, L. A. 1987. How to Make Time Work for You. *Parade Magazine*. May: 4-5.

Webster's New Riverside Dictionary. 1996. Boston: Houghton Mifflin.

Weinraub, Judith. 2003. The Power of the Pyramid. *Washington Post*. January 15, F1, F5.

Wells, Doris T. 2003. Reducing Stress for Officers and Their Families. *Corrections Today*. Vol. 65, No. 2, April, pp. 24-25.

Whisenand, Paul M. and R. Fred Ferguson. 2002. *The Managing of Police Organizations*. Upper Saddle River, New Jersey: Prentice Hall.

Whitehead, John T. 1989. *Burnout in Probation and Corrections*. New York: Praeger.

Whiteman, Thomas, Sam Verghese, and Randy Petersen. 1996. *The Complete Stress Management Workbook*. Grand Rapids: Zondervan.

Whittlesey, M. 1986. *Stress*. Springhouse, Pennsylvania: Springhouse, American Family Institute.

Willet, Walter C., M.D. 2001. *Eat, Drink and Be Healthy: The Harvard Medical School Guide to Healthy Eating*. New York: The Free Press.

Witkin-Lanoil, G. 1986. *The Male Stress Syndrome*. New York: Berkeley.

Wood, P. 1985. Eat More, Play More—Weigh Less. *Reader's Digest*. 135, May: 125-29.

Woodruff, L. 1993. Occupational Stress for Correctional Personnel: What The Research Indicates. *American Jails*. September-October: 15-20.

Zupan, L., R. Conroy, and W. J. Smith. 1991. Officer Stress in the Direct Supervision Jail. *American Jails*. November-December: 35-36.

About the Author

Lt. Gary F. Cornelius has just retired from the Fairfax County Sheriff's Office where he had served since 1978. He has more than twenty-five years of experience in law enforcement and corrections. He has a Bachelor of Arts degree in Social Sciences from Edinboro University of Pennsylvania, and is a former officer of the Uniformed Division of the U.S. Secret Service. In his correctional career, Gary has worked in many areas of jail operations, and before his retirement was the Classification Supervisor of the Fairfax County Adult Detention Center. Lt. Cornelius also teaches punishment and corrections and community corrections at George Mason University, and has been an adjunct faculty member there since 1986. He has taught many seminars on various subjects in corrections for the past fifteen years and is a certified trainer for the Virginia Department of Criminal Justice Services.

Lt. Cornelius is active as a trainer and consultant for the National Institute of Justice, the American Jail Association, the American Correctional Association, and the International Association of Correctional Training Personnel (IACTP). In 1997, he was elected to the IACTP Board and represents local corrections training. He is on the Board of Advisors of *The Corrections Professional* from LRP Publications. He has written more than forty articles on corrections, including a quarterly column, now a book, called *The Twenty Minute Trainer*. His other books include *The Correctional Trainer* and *The Correctional Officer: A Practical Guide*. He has written for the American Correctional Association: *Jails in America: An Overview of Issues, 2nd Edition*, and *The Art of the Con: Avoiding Offender Manipulation*, which was the recipient of the 2002 APEX (Award for Publication Excellence) award by Communications Concepts. All of his books are available from the American Correctional Association.

He has served as a consultant on the National Institute of Justice report: *Addressing Correctional Officer Stress: Programs and Strategies, an Issues and Practices Report*. In 2001, Lt. Cornelius received the IACTP Board of Directors' Award of Excellence in Correctional Training and the IACTP President's Award in 2004. He is included in the

1992-1993 edition of *Who's Who among Human Service Professionals*. In 2001 he was named to *America's Registry of Outstanding Professionals*. He is a native of Pittsburgh, Pennsylvania and resides with his family in Fairfax, Virginia.

The ABC's of Offender Management

Correctional Law for the Correctional Officer, 4th Edition

William C. Collins, J.D.

This updated edition answers officers' questions about the rights of inmates and staff, and provides correctional staff with a basic understanding of the law. Includes federal and state court cases. Explains legal liabilities and rights associated with searches and seizures, use of force, punishment, AIDS, suicide, protective custody, religion, mail, visitation, and more. This edition includes review questions and answers for each chapter. (2004, 252 pages, 1-56991-066-9)

The Art of the Con: Avoiding Offender Manipulation

Gary F. Cornelius

In many instances, correctional staff believe they are too smart to be manipulated by an offender. Realizing this possibility exists is the first step to avoiding it. This book provides the corrections professional with a better understanding of offenders and their characteristics, behavior and culture. It shows how staff and volunteers can maintain authority and control by resisting manipulation. Cornelius includes examples to improve the learning curve. The concepts in this book apply to anyone in the field, and show how manipulation can occur in prisons, jails or community supervision. (2001, 128 pages, 1-56991-147-9)

Building A Stronger Career In Corrections